Attraction and Attachment: Understanding Styles of Relationships

Attraction and Attachment: Understanding Styles of Relationships

Barbara Jo Brothers
Editor

Routledge
Taylor & Francis Group
New York London

Routledge is an imprint of the
Taylor & Francis Group, an informa business

Attraction and Attachment: Understanding Styles of Relationships has also been published as *Journal of Couples Therapy*, Volume 4, Numbers 1/2 1993.

The development, preparation, and publication of this work has been undertaken with great care. However, the publisher, employees, editors, and agents of The Haworth Press and all imprints of The Haworth Press, Inc., including The Haworth Medical Press and Pharmaceutical Products Press, are not responsible for any errors contained herein or for consequences that may ensue from use of materials or information contained in this work. Opinions expressed by the author(s) are not necessarily those of The Haworth Press, Inc.

Reprinted 2009 by Routledge

Library of Congress Cataloging-in-Publication Data

Attraction and attachment : understanding styles of relationships /
    Barbara Jo Brothers, editor.
        p. cm.
    "Attraction and attachment has also been published as Journal of couples therapy, volume 4, numbers 1/2, 1993"–T.p. verso.
    Includes bibliographical references.
    ISBN 1-56024-620-0 (alk. paper)
    1. Man-woman relationships. 2. Marriages. 3. Marital psychotherapy. I. Brothers, Barbara, 1940– .
HQ801.A825 1993   93-42448
306.81–dc20   CIP

Attraction and Attachment: Understanding Styles of Relationships

CONTENTS

ABOUT THE EDITOR

Barbara Jo Brothers, MSW, BCD, a Diplomate in Clinical Social Work, National Association of Social Workers, is in private practice in New Orleans. She received her BA from the University of Texas and her MSW from Tulane University, where she is currently on the faculty. She was Editor of *The Newsletter of the American Academy of Psychotherapists* from 1976 to 1985, and was Associate Editor of *Voices: The Art and Science of Psychotherapy* from 1979 to 1989. She has nearly 30 years of experience, in both the public and private sectors, helping people to form skills that will enable them to connect emotionally. The author of numerous articles and book chapters on authenticity in human relating, she has advocated healthy, congruent communication that builds intimacy as opposed to destructive, incongruent communication which blocks intimacy. In addition to her many years of direct work with couples and families, Ms. Brothers has led numerous workshops on teaching communication in families and has also played an integral role in the development of training programs in family therapy for mental health workers throughout the Louisiana state mental health system. She is a board member of the Institute for International Connections, a non-profit organization for cross-cultural professional development focused on training and cross-cultural exchange with psychotherapists in Russia, republics once part of what used to be the Soviet Union, and other Eastern European countries.

Balance and Attachment
and–Sometimes–Love

Barbara Jo Brothers

Love does not take you off balance.

–Virginia Satir, July 12, 1968

SUMMARY. A brief discussion of balance in family systems and various forms of attachment between couples observed by Virginia Satir; "Six Ways of Making 'Us.'" Illustrations are included.

As therapists, we all know there is much in this world that passes for love and has far more to do with leftover dependency needs and unresolved attachment issues. The person in chronic disharmony within herself or himself is, emotionally, in no position to be in harmony with a partner unless both partners are much more aware of their respective inner selves than most people are inclined to be. Thus, they seek blindly to bring their system into balance and they make the desperate thrust for attachment, rather than the discovery of loving connection.

As I thought about those various forms of "love impostors" and this volume's theme–"Attractions and Attachments"–I remem-

[Haworth co-indexing entry note]: "Balance and Attachment and–Sometimes–Love," Brothers, Barbara Jo. Co-published simultaneously in the *Journal of Couples Therapy* (The Haworth Press, Inc.) Vol. 4, No. 1/2, 1993, pp. 1-11; and: *Attraction and Attachment: Understanding Styles of Relationships* (ed: Barbara Jo Brothers) The Haworth Press, Inc., 1993, pp. 1-11. Multiple copies of this article/chapter may be purchased from The Haworth Document Delivery Center [1-800-3-HAWORTH; 9:00 a.m. - 5:00 p.m. (EST)].

bered Virginia Satir speaking about these matters in terms of *balance* in family systems:

> All families work toward wholeness, [but] probably the balance is going to require terrible things, a terrible price . . . We have to think of balance as what price does each part [of the system] play in order to keep the balance . . . If one part pays more than another part, then the thing is destructive . . . what price do you pay in order to "keep a balance?" Some of us have paid half of our lives for a balance so we shouldn't disturb anybody . . . (1982, p.73)

> Balance is achieved at too big a price, for one part is against another. Backs hurt and genitals don't work and all kinds of other stuff in relation to this. (1982, p.126)

Virginia's definition of "mental health" (a term of which she was not particularly fond, but used here for want of a better one) was a behavioral one: to achieve it, people would (1) give up static, stylized–and, therefore, "unhealthy" responses for coping with their self doubt, (2) learn to honor their feelings as a step in honoring their own identity, (3) then chose, instead, authentic responses that fit the given occasion.

In a couple of the earliest Satir workshops that I attended, Virginia presented her observations about relationships between couples, using her now well-known method of placing volunteer role players from the audience in sculpted body positions. "Six Ways of Making 'Us' "[1] was how she captioned her discussion of styles of relationship among couples. As I had found the images very useful through the years, I have included, in the next few pages, my own illustrations from my notes taken at the workshops. (See Figures 1-6.) I have not found them indexed, as such, in any of the major works that present her model.

---

1. Virginia Satir. Speaker: July, 1968. Week-long seminar sponsored by NASW Southern Regional Institute, Biloxi, Mississippi; August 1971. Month-long seminar sponsored by the Evergreen Institute, Evergreen, Colorado. Except for a very brief, unlabeled, description of "the drag" and reference to "victim/ victimizer" under "Positive Pairing" in *The New Peoplemaking*, p. 326, these "six ways" do not appear in the books on the Satir model.

Her point was that all six of the illustrated ways inhibit independent action and growth and mitigate against "standing on one's own two feet." In all six, the balance of one depends on the other.

SIX WAYS OF MAKING 'US'

Siamese Twins: this is the symbiotic relationship wherein it seems that neither member of the pair can take a step without the other; it may *look* like they are separate people, but they share a common backbone. "Siamese Twins" can be performed by people

FIGURE 1. SIAMESE TWINS

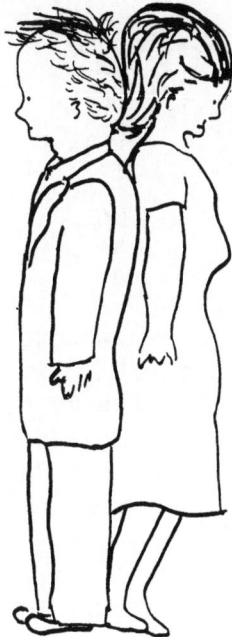

FIGURE 2. SUFFOCATION

whose stress response is super-reasonable (Satir, 1988, 1991) when the emphasis is more on "head" than "heart." There would be a lack of emotional connection if they were to move apart.

Suffocation: a variation of the symbiotic relationship, but with more intensity of feeling and less "room to breathe." "You are my whole world"; mutual placation prevails.

Leaning on Each Other: a mutually dependent stance where each person would topple if the other made an independent move; it looks like space between them, but contact is rather meager.

The Drag: can be seen in "old-fashioned" marriages where the husband is head of the household and "takes care of" the woman; can be seen in marriages where the long-suffering wife "takes care of" the alcoholic husband.

FIGURE 3. LEANING ON EACH OTHER

Victim/Victimizer: husbands "hen-pecked" by wives and wives battered by husbands are two ends of a continuum of this position.

Adoration: one of the members of the couple put the other on a pedestal; generally, there is no sex between them—they are together for "spiritual" reasons.

It was Virginia's ambition to free couples from the static, reflex defensive responses to their pain by giving them access to their own inner resources. She believed deeply in the essential value of every human being. For her, a person was a marvel, a unique creation in the cosmos. She wanted to give back to each family member with whom she worked, the gift of his/her own self which would provide the energy and motivation for that person taking active charge of her/his own life.

FIGURE 4. THE DRAG

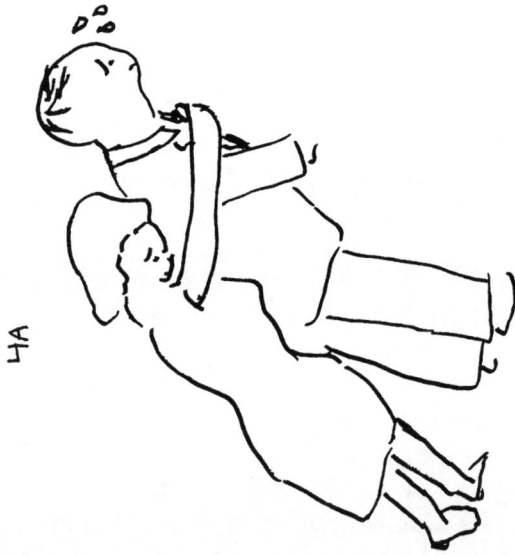

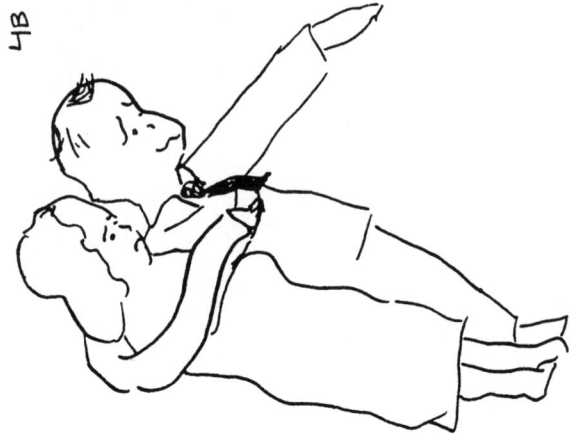

4B

4A

FIGURE 5. VICTIM/VICTIMIZER

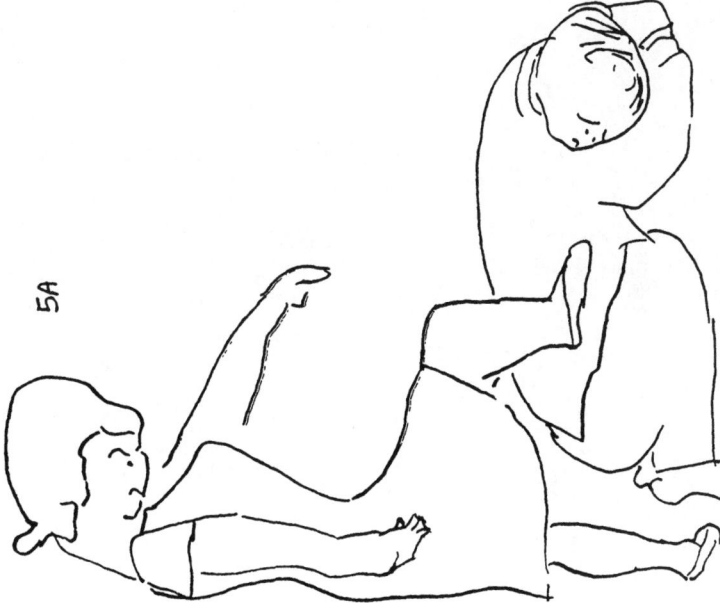

5A

5B

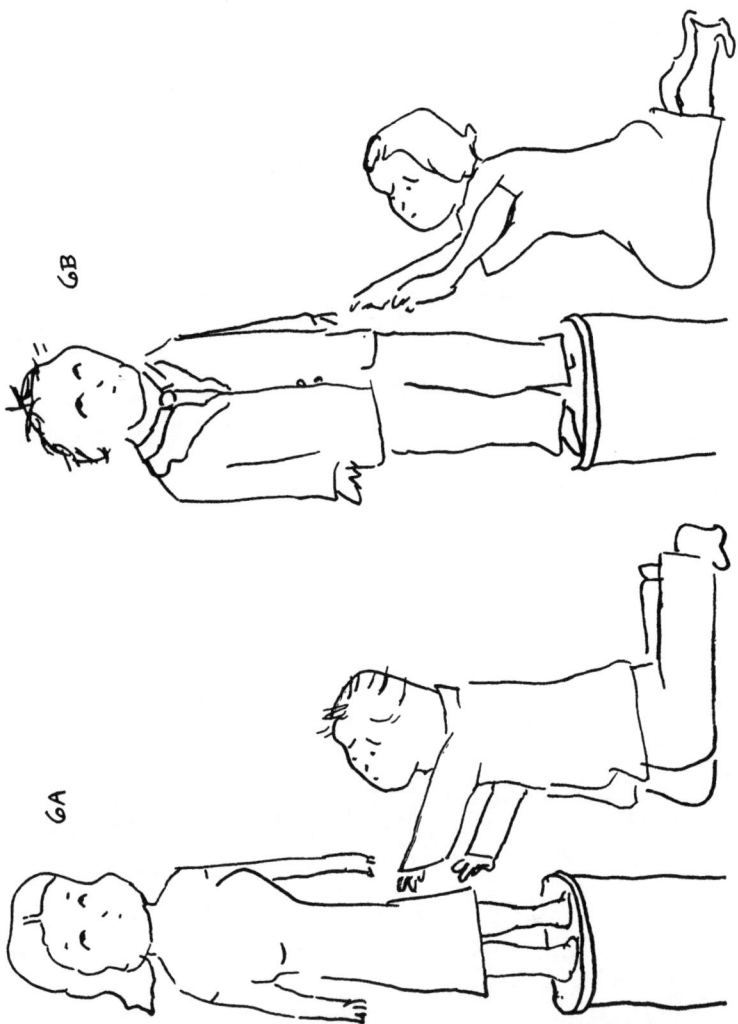

FIGURE 6. So-Called "SPIRITUAL" RELATIONSHIP

6A

6B

. . . There are pieces we need to retrieve that will help us to move to where we can be what I call in charge of our own life. Another way of talking about it is to take our life in our own hands. Another way of talking about it is to become a co-creator of our life force. (Satir and Banmen, 1983, p. 333)

Long years of working with families had shown Virginia that those who labored to model themselves after images of how they "ought to" be and "should" be were seriously diminishing their chances of *authentically* being their own person. She invented her family reconstruction and parts party vehicles as ways of helping family members see the origins of their "shoulds" and "oughts."

Virginia's bone deep respect for people, *all* people, was the real "moving force" behind her success. She understood the great healing power that comes with mutual respect and mutual understanding. Understanding this power, Virginia designed her "meditations" to help bring the person *into* balance *before* she or he entered into interaction with another. In her earlier days, she called them "centering exercises." The purpose of the following exercise, which took place in her third month-long Process Community Seminar, was to help build a context conducive to making connections between people; she considered such a context essential for both the learning process as well as the growth process:

. . . and let the tension go out on an outgoing breath . . . And let yourself further become aware that you are safe and secure in your chair, and feel your body, your feet on the ground and your bottom on the chair, your back pressing against the back, giving you that solid support. And let yourself further become aware that your feet, resting on the floor, are not only supported by the floor, but by the energy that comes from the center of the universe, coming up through your feet and legs and into your body, being your source of groundedness . . . This energy is forever available for people through the day, all day long, all of the time that you live and breathe on this planet . . . It is only for your awareness to be in touch [that is required], and you take advantage of the energy. Energy of groundedness that comes from the center of the earth. Let yourself become aware of the energy from the heavens, as it moves down through the top of your head into your face and neck, arms and chest, meeting the energy of groundedness . . . That energy from the heavens, the energy of inspiration, of sensing, of imagination, the place where all the real imaging is grounded. And as the energy of intuition, [of] inspiration, of sensing meets the energy of groundedness, it forms still a third energy. And the energy of intuition, imagination and sensing is also forever there. It waits only for you to acknowledge access to it. And as these two energies mingle together, the third energy they create is the energy of connectedness with another human being, the energy that flows out through your arms and skin and eyes, facial expression, to other persons, creating the bonding, the joy, the possibilities of building with other people . . . I'd just like you to become aware that you have energies like a three-legged stool, energies from this connectedness, your intuition . . . Energies which create a *balance* of yourself . . . (Satir and Banmen, 1983, pp. 1 & 2)

Of course, the "seventh way" of making "us" that takes place between two people who *are* able to maintain their separate balances can not be illustrated and may only be experienced; it is a living, in-the-moment response that is appropriate to whatever is going on in the context and within the hearts of the two people in interaction at the given point in time.

Virginia made use of many different routes to help a given couple or family move toward this balance of energies. The first step was to bring into awareness in each individual in the system a sense of her or his own worth; this would facilitate a sense of balance from *within*–"peace within" as she called it in the last several years of her life (1987). Only when the separate selves within a system could perceive themselves as centered would a constructive connection with another be possible. Mutual respect between two people follows respect for the *self* within each. Two persons might then exist–not in symbiotic bonds, not as burdens to each other, not attacking each other, or distancing each other–but in creative *connection* with each other. This was what Virginia meant in speaking of "peace between." Virginia Satir's extended vision included the possibility that such balance, coming as a result of mutual, deep respect, could also occur in the larger "family system," the family of humankind. This is what she meant when she spoke of "peace among."

REFERENCES

Satir, V. (Speaker). (1982, August). Lecture presented at Process Community II, Crested Butte, Colorado.

Satir, V. & Banmen, J. (1983). *Virginia Satir verbatim 1984.* Transcription of Process Community III, 1983, Crested Butte, Colorado. (Available from Delta Psychological Services, 11213 Canyon Crescent, N. Delta, British Columbia, Canada, V4E2R6.)

Satir, V. (Speaker). (1987, October). [Videotape]. International Human Learning Resources Network. October Meeting. Hacienda Vista Hermosa, Cuernavaca, Mexico. (Available from Morris Gordon, 3705 George Mason Dr. #C35, Falls Church, Virginia 22041).

Satir, V. (1988). *The new peoplemaking.* Mountain View, California: Science and Behavior Books.

Satir, V., Banmen, J., Gerber, J., Gomori, M. (1991). The *Satir model.* Mountain View, California: Science and Behavior Books.

Marriage and Attachment:
An Exploration of Ten Long-Term Marriages

Alyce Jackson

SUMMARY. Attachment behavior (Bowlby, 1969) is considered an integral part of intimate human relating throughout the life span. This research examined the recollections of ten happy couples in long-term marriages as to their attachment experiences in childhood, and their current attachment experiences in marriage. The findings indicated that none of these happily married subjects were raised in homes where both parents were physically and emotionally available. Yet, in adult life they had clearly succeeded in establishing fulfilling long-term relationships. These findings suggested that attachment behavior is subject to modification throughout the life cycle and is not rigidly fixed in childhood. The data suggested that insight, changes in the parent/subject relationship, and the marital relationship were some of the primary factors which could account for the changes in attachment behavior.

Children learn what they live. Do childhood attachments, however, serve as models for intimate relationships in adulthood? Proponents of continuity argue that a person's emotional development during childhood serves as a template which both structures and increasingly restricts future affective functioning. Opponents posit that discontinuity rather than permanence characterizes intrapsychic and interpersonal development. Are individuals who are success-

[Haworth co-indexing entry note]: "Marriage and Attachment: An Exploration of Ten Long-Term Marriages," Jackson, Alyce. Co-published simultaneously in the *Journal of Couples Therapy* (The Haworth Press, Inc.) Vol. 4, No. 1/2, 1993, pp. 13-30; and: *Attraction and Attachment: Understanding Styles of Relationships* (ed: Barbara Jo Brothers) The Haworth Press, Inc., 1993, pp. 13-30. Multiple copies of this article/chapter may be purchased from The Haworth Document Delivery Center [1-800-3-HAWORTH; 9:00 a.m. - 5:00 p.m. (EST)].

fully married in long-term relationships the products of happy homes whose current adult functioning is the repetition of earlier family of origin experiences? If happily married spouses were raised in environments which were less than optimal where and how did they learn to form mutually satisfying attachments?

OVERVIEW OF RESULTS

The research on which this article is based explored the attachment histories as well as the current attachment experiences of currently married adults. Ten happy couples in long-term marriages (mean = 27 years) who were nominated by clergy and mental health professionals and screened with the Dyadic Adjustment Scale (Spanier, 1976) were interviewed in depth using a semi-structured inventory. Eight major themes of attachment were explored: availability, understanding, separation and reunion behavior, loss, support receiving, support giving, and autonomy.

What were the subjects' recollections of their early attachment experiences? How did they describe their marital relationships? The results will be briefly summarized due to space restraints. Eighteen subjects grew up in homes where at least one parent was physically available. None of the subjects experienced a parental death during childhood, nor were any of them separated from their caretakers for an indeterminate period of time. Nine participants indicated that one parent provided understanding and compassion during childhood. In adulthood, however, 18 subjects had at least one relationship which enabled them to feel understood. As children, eight subjects turned to others when they felt emotionally distressed. Yet, in adult life, 16 subjects turned to their spouses when they felt upset, and all of them attempted to provide support to their partners when needed. While 14 subjects described themselves as compliant children, all of the spouses indicated that their marital relationship included reciprocal tolerance of autonomous ideas and/or behaviors.

The data from these categories revealed some striking differences between childhood and adult life. Despite the fact that the subjects were all happily married, none of them described an "Ozzie and Harriet" type childhood home life where both parents were physically and emotionally available. Similarly, none of the subjects described both of their parents as understanding although 45% of the sample indicated that one parent provided understanding during childhood. In adult life, on the other hand, 15/20 subjects reported feeling understood by their spouses. In seven couples, there was a reciprocal relationship where each perceived the other as a primary source of comprehension and compassion.

How does one make sense of the findings? How is it that subjects who came from less than ideal circumstances were able to develop satisfying family lives, and in most instances have more successful marital relationships than those reported of their parents? If internal working models of self and other formed during childhood guide intimate relating throughout the life span, how does one understand the discrepancy between the subjects' graphically detailed childhood remembrances and their current experiences in adult life? Bowlby, after all did note that ". . . whatever expectations are developed during those years tend to persist relatively unchanged throughout the rest of life" (1973, p. 238). This article will examine some of the results through the lenses of two major schools of thought: continuity and discontinuity in human development.

CONTINUITY

We may our ends by our beginnings know

Bowlby's (1979) work supported the extension of attachment theory from childhood to adult love and loss. Although Bowlby did speak about the ways in which developmental pathways could be modified, the bulk of his work focused on the personality's tendency, through self-regulation, to maintain its current direction of development. ". . . and on those [internal] models are based all of his expectations, and therefore all his plans, for the rest of his life" (1973, p. 369). He contended that "attachment behavior characterizes human beings from the cradle to the grave" (p. 40). Similarly, Ainsworth posited that "there are and can be other significant attachments in the life span: husband to wife, wife to husband, . . . close friend to close friend to name a few" (1972, p. 101).

Bowlby's contention that inner working models are highly resistant to change has also received significant theoretical and empirical support. Fairbairn and others suggested that the intertwining of an adult's internal representations of the self and the attachment figure has a pervasive effect on the individual's thinking and interpersonal behavior (Cohen, 1974, p. 216). Chess, Thomas, Korn, Mittelman, and Cohen's (1983) research supports the continuity position. In their New York longitudinal study they found that there was a significant correlation between an assessment of marital conflict taken when the subjects' children were 3 years old and a measure of the children's adult adaptation taken when they were 18 to 22 years old.

The Berkeley Growth Study (Elder, 1979; Caspi and Elder, 1987), another longitudinal investigation, also supported this contention. Using initially retrospective reports from the parents of the first children studied, the researchers found that growing up in families in which the parental care was viewed as unaffectionate, hostile, and controlling was associated with the development of personal instabilities that were reflected in tension in the marital relationship and extreme and arbitrary discipline shown towards their own children. The children of these individuals (the third generation) themselves were likely to develop problems as adults, the women being described by their own children (the fourth generation) as ill tempered and by their husbands as explosive in child rearing (Dunn, 1988, p. 200). Similarly, Brooks (1981) concluded that children raised in warm consistent environments later raised adolescents who were socially and emotionally integrated and thus likely to replicate their early environments when they married and had children. How prevalent was continuity in the sample we studied?

In this study, nine of the twenty subjects described attachment patterns in adulthood that are congruent with the ones they reported in childhood. For example, these subjects were asked what they did when they were emotionally upset during childhood and adulthood. They responded that they turned to a parent or spouse.

Mr. Erikson, who has been married for 21 years, provides perhaps the clearest example of continuity of support seeking or attachment behavior. During his childhood he turned to his father for understanding and assistance. In adulthood,

> . . . I will always discuss it with my wife and get her feedback on it. Sometimes as a sounding board, sometimes to get her

advice, opinion, recommendation for action. . . . [She has always been] supportive of my endeavors professionally, supportive of me as a person. Like in the way that my father was ... about taking my side on things. ... I mean obviously if I am wrong she is going to be supportive of me emotionally, but point out to me that I might have done something or other to screw things up. In that sense [she] has always been a very good truthsayer to me.

Congruency or continuity, of course, indicates that those subjects who did not turn to others during childhood continued that pattern in adulthood. That was borne out by the results of this study. Mr. Tourosian's (married 34 years) observation illustrates the point.

I would keep to myself. I still do that. I have a habit of not communicating if I feel something is wrong or a situation arises. I generally don't like to pass the problem off. I try to resolve it myself, or stew over it myself, or let it resolve by itself. I still have that habit which is not good and is probably one of the reasons why I had a heart attack.

DISCONTINUITY

Although Bowlby wrote at length about the formation of inner working models and their tendency to persist throughout the life span, he never contended that once established an attachment pattern was irrevocably fixed. In his last book (1988), citing recent research, he focused more on the etiology of developmental change. He employed the construct of developmental pathways to explicate his view that people are continuously shaped by past experiences and current interactions with their environments. Current experiences can, thus, modify the individual's course or pathway.

This means that it is necessary to think of each personality as moving through life along some developmental pathway, with the pathway followed always being determined by the interaction of the personality as it has so far developed and the environment in which it is then finding itself. (1988 p. 172)

In the last book he authored before his death Bowlby wrote about change throughout the life span. He indicated that it was a human being's inherent ability to change that laid at the heart of therapy.

> Although the capacity for developmental change diminishes with age, change continues throughout the life cycle so that changes for better or for worse are always possible. It is this continuing potential for change that means that at no point in life is a person invulnerable to possible adversity and also that at no point in life is a person impermeable to favourable influence. It is this persisting potential for change that gives opportunity for effective therapy. (1988, p. 136)

His belief that early attachment patterns can be altered is echoed by Belsky and Nezworski (1988).

> If the nature and the quality of care provided to the child is changed and/or the child's or *adult's* [italics added] working model of self and of relationships is modified, then according to attachment theory we should expect that developmental outcomes anticipated on the basis of early assessments of attachment security should not necessarily emerge. Although such contextual and/or personal changes may be difficult to evoke, they are presumed not only to be possible but also to have predictable outcomes. Indeed, under the right conditions, one might anticipate change in developmental trajectories and thus appropriately speak of "lawful discontinuity." (p. 14)

Bowlby cited Brown and Harris's (1978) research to amplify his point. Their study compared depressed women versus controls in inner London, outer London, and the Scottish highlands. Brown and Harris (1978) identified four variables which appeared significantly more frequently among depressed members of the population. Three of these variables involved *current* events and circumstances. The first was a severe unfortunate event which typically involved an important personal loss or disappointment. This event usually occurred during the year prior to the beginning of the depression. The second variable was the absence of a companion to whom the subject could confide. The third variable was chronically difficult living conditions. Only the fourth variable was a historical one. It was a woman's loss of her mother due to death or prolonged separation before her eleventh birthday (Bowlby, 1988, p. 174).

While it is unlikely that any of the subjects studied were familiar with the theoretical and empirical support for discontinuity, many of them undoubtedly would agree with its existence. Fifty five percent of the subjects described childhood attachment behaviors which were not congruent with their described reactions as adults. Ten of these 11 subjects who did not remember or did not turn to others when upset as a child, did so as adults.

It is doubtful that Bowlby would label more than half of the sample "the exception to the rule." What phenomenon could explain the outcome? Perhaps the sample was too small. While it is likely that the percentage of people describing incongruent childhood and adult attachment behaviors might change in a larger sample, it, of course, is unclear to what degree and in what direction.

INSIGHT AND CHANGE

Those who can not remember the past are doomed to repeat it

–George Santayana

Bowlby's (1973) contention that once formed inner working models are intractable to change was based on his premise that they operate outside of the individual's awareness. He also posited that if people became aware of their deepest beliefs about self and other they could choose to maintain them or, if viewed as dysfunctional, modify their beliefs and behavior. Bowlby posited that this process, along with the therapeutic relationship, was the crux of psychotherapy. He addressed the topic of therapeutic change.

> Thus, the patient is encouraged to believe that, with support and occasional guidance, he can discover for himself the true nature of the models that underlie his thoughts, feelings, and actions and that, by examining the nature of his earlier experiences with his parents, or parent substitutes, he will understand what has led him to build the models now active within

him and *thus be free to restructure them* [Italics added]. Fortunately the human psyche, like human bones, is strongly inclined towards self-healing. (1988 p. 152)

He also believed that people have the capability of assessing their internal models with little professional psychological interpretation. For Bowlby, the essence of psychotherapy was that the answer lies within.

Bowlby cited Main, Kaplan, and Cassidy's (1985) research to support his contention that individuals who had free emotional and cognitive access to their internal models could improve their mental health. Main et al. found a strong correlation between how a mother described her relationships with her parents during her childhood and the pattern of attachment her child currently had with her. "Whereas the mother of a secure infant is able to talk freely and with feeling about her childhood, the mother of an insecure infant is not" (Bowlby, 1988, p. 133). Adults were evaluated after being administered the Adult Attachment Interview. Subjects who were identified as "secure" valued attachment relationships, exhibited readiness of recall, and lacked idealization of parents or of past experiences. Subjects who were identified as avoidant lacked those characteristics.

The finding that Bowlby found particularly germane was one which he described as an exception to the "general rule." The researchers focused on mothers who described unhappy childhoods but were able to raise children who appeared to be securely attached. They discovered that a characteristic of these women which differentiated them from the mothers of insecure infants was the womens' ability to relate balanced accounts of their childhoods. While the women were frequently upset during the interview, they were coherent and included both positive and negative aspects of their childhoods and their relationships with their parents. Main did not posit that it was necessary that the subject had "forgiven" their parents for past transgressions. It was sufficient that the subject was able to coherently discuss their ambivalent feelings and to some degree recognize their parents as part of the human condition. The researchers concluded "that free access to, and the coherent organization of information relevant to attachment play a determining role in the development of a secure personality in adult life" (Bowlby, 1988, p. 135).

All of the current research subjects spoke about how their childhood experiences impacted on their adult lives. They showed remarkable insight into their parents' assets and deficiencies as role models as well as their own strengths and weaknesses. The major theme which emerged from this process was the subjects' perceptions that their parents had done the best they could. Understanding, accepting, and forgiving one's parents were threads that were interwoven throughout the interviews.

This type of "working through" or cognitive and emotional integration of childhood material is indicative of people who have recognized their histories and, thus, escape the condemnation to repeat them. Not surprisingly, the subjects who had been in therapy had given the matter a great deal of thought. As Bowlby (1988) suggested, this awareness and integration allows for the formation of modified models and paradigms for intimate relating with spouses and children.

Several of the discontinuous subjects reported that they used their childhood relationships as negative models to serve as a springboard for healthier contemporary relationships. Another discontinuity that emerged was changes perceptions. Mr. Oppenheimer who has been married for 34 years stated:

> My mother sort of reflected what she herself had been taught. . . . I suppose the only thing that has changed is that I have finally come to the realization that I am not going to change her, and I ought to stop trying. My attitude has changed considerably. She doesn't have that many years left so I might as well make them as comfortable and pleasing as possible.

Six subjects spoke about the impact of their parents' marriages on their current marital relationship. Five of them "learned by the negative," that is by either doing the opposite of what their parents did or consciously living in a very different way. Mrs. Oppenheimer, for example, reflected:

> I don't think that the marriage between my mother and my father was particularly happy to tell you the truth. It sounds like everything was wonderful. I don't think they had much of

a relationship. I think they were almost like two worlds, and they would intersect occasionally, but I don't think they communicated that well between the two of them to tell you the truth . . . I did not want to replicate that kind of situation. So I think in some ways I learned from the negative.

Another theoretical perspective which sheds light on the continuity/discontinuity issue is the interpersonal perspective.

THE INTERPERSONAL CONTEXT FOR CHANGE

Epstein (cited in Ricks, 1985) posited that representational or inner working models change as a consequence of lawful processes. First, change occurs in the context of emotional experience. While Epstein acknowledged that emotionally significant events may not result in representational modification because of situational factors or individual differences, he posited that change is unlikely to occur in the absence of emotion. Second, he hypothesized that if attachment bonds are acquired via the internalization of early interpersonal experiences, modification occurs in the context of three major types of emotionally corrective interpersonal experiences:

> through change within the same early relationship across time, through repeated experience in other relationships that disconfirm earlier acquired models, and through especially strong emotional experience within a single relationship that similarly disconfirms earlier postulates. Since models of self and other are complementary, reflected appraisals from others that differ from childhood appraisals are particularly significant. . . . the implicit logic behind naturally occurring changes in self-esteem is as follows: 'I admire this person; he likes and respects me. Then maybe I am a worthwhile person myself; after all, I respect his judgement.' (p. 227)

Several of the participants indicated that their relationships with their parents had changed significantly over the course of the subjects' adulthoods. Those subjects whose parents are still alive spoke in terms of their current relationships. Some of the subjects described how their interactions with and attitudes toward their parents shifted as the latter became elderly and confronted death. Mrs. Stanford (married 11 years) spoke about her current relationship with her mother and father.

> I am really happy with [my relationship with my parents as an adult]. Since my dad retired we are really having conversations. . . . There was that time when we didn't talk that much [college and young adulthood], and then I think when I finally decided to have kids and could share that, being pregnant, my mom and I talked about it a lot. That was the beginning of us getting back on course together and sharing experiences as an adult. I really felt like we could be adults together. . . . I know there are things they don't like about what we do. . . . I feel really fortunate. I take them for granted.

Several subjects reported that their relationships with their parents had changed dramatically over time disconfirming to some degree their "earlier acquired models" (Epstein cited in Ricks, 1985). In addition, all of the subjects experienced a strong emotional experience within the single relationship of marriage. Two possible consequences of "a strong emotional experience within a single relationship" are altered self-perception and increased self-esteem. Thus, as we shall see in the next section, the subjects' improved relationships with their parents may in part have been due to the impact of the subjects' marriages on themselves and their perceptions of others.

THE ROLE OF MARRIAGE

[The marriage] has been therapeutic, and corrective, and a godsend. It's more than made up for my slow start in life. God knew just what I needed.

–Mrs. Walton

Mrs. Walton's analysis of the role marriage has played in her life has significant theoretical and empirical support. Mattison and Sinclair (1979), Napier and Whitaker (1978), Kirschner and Kirschner (1986), and others have posited that marriage offers individuals a second chance to form an attachment relationship. They also believe that for many individuals the marital relationship can ameliorate, at least in part, the effects of earlier less satisfying relationships.

The Kirschners (1986) posited that in all marriages there is a natural drive to create a healing relationship, one that not only replicates, but also transcends transactional gestalts that the spouses experienced in their families of origin. Mattison and Sinclair (1979) expressed a similar concept. "Marriage holds the promise of being able to make better what was felt to be wrong in the past and to make partnership more satisfying than is dimly remembered from childhood" (p. 52).

Mr. Oppenheimer and Mrs. Walton (married 28 years) indicated that, at least in their lives, this was indeed the case.

> I think if anything my childhood experiences had a positive impact because I am aware of the fact that things perhaps did not go as I wished they had gone, and I think in many ways I have compensated for that. I think I compensate in my relations with my wife and certainly in my relations with my children.
>
> –Mr. Oppenheimer

> I think some of the things that happened to me I used to reverse . . . My husband was the complete antithesis of what I grew up with which was what perhaps drew me to him initially . . . I never had any affirmation. My husband affirms me more than I affirm him . . . I think he knows that I didn't get that as a kid so he does it a lot.
>
> –Mrs. Walton

Mr. White, who was married 12 years, believed that his relationship with his wife has had a positive effect on his physical and psychological well being.

> Whether [my wife] is a substitute for my mother or not I don't know. When I met my wife I was taking a prescription of Lib-

rium for a spastic colon which was totally anxiety related. . . . I'd say the wedding was the last time I had any. I don't feel there is any risk of getting back in that scenario with the possible exception of losing one of my immediate family.

The Kirschners' (1986) described how marriage, a "strong emotional relationship," fosters change. The Kirschners believe that attachment is one of the primary needs throughout the life cycle. They posited that spouses transfer their attachment needs from their parents to each another in the beginning of marriage.

> In a regressive burst, termed falling in love, mates idealize their partners in a manner resembling that of a young child with a parent. This process sets the stage for each spouse to accept the other's suggestions and ideas about himself or herself and the nature of reality, much as a child does with a parent. The new bond replaces the old parental relationship and thus promotes individuation from the family, one of the first tasks of marriage. (1986, p. 4)

There is also empirical support for the belief that stable marriages improve mental health and buffer the individuals involved from at least some of the deleterious effects of stress (Dunn, 1988, p. 198). Kotler's (1985) research indicated that strong marital relations were therapeutic for a partner whose early experiences of care were less than optimal. Kotler and Omodei (1988) found that later marital quality was strongly related to the mental health of both partners. Similarly, Gove, Hughes, and Style (1983) posited that ". . . it is the quality of a marriage and not marriage per se that links marriage to positive mental health" (p. 122). Valliant's (1977) longitudinal research concluded that the variable which best predicted mental health was the subject's capacity to remain happily married over time. Egeland, Jacobvitz and Stroufe (1988) discovered that an emotionally supportive, satisfying marriage helped women who were abused during childhood to break the cycle of abuse when raising their own children. Rutter and Quinton (1984) echoed their results. In *Long-term follow-up of women institutionalized in childhood: Factors promoting good functioning in adult life* they stated that "the findings . . . suggested that the spouses' good qualities exerted a powerful ameliorating effect leading to an increased likelihood of good psychosocial functioning and a decreased likelihood of personality disorder." The researchers empirically proved that the positive effects could not be attributed to assortative mating or the effect of the women on their spouses.

A majority of the studies focused on how stable or happy marriages prove to be beneficial for women. Can the same be said for men? Gove, Hughes and Style (1983) stated that while the affective quality of the marriage is more important for females, marital status alone is important for males. It is probably safe to assume, therefore, that the benefits of a supportive marital union will accrue to men as well as women.

The Minnesota (Morris, 1980; 1981), Berkeley (Main and Goldwyn, 1984), and Amherst (Ricks, 1985) studies also found that good child outcome was associated with mothers who lived in stable marriages and had positive self-esteem despite having been raised themselves in families where they experienced either rejection or abandonment. These women often had exceptionally strong ties to their husband's families which also served to ameliorate their childhood deficits.

While all of the subjects did not explicitly talk about how their marriages have effected their mental health, all of the subjects indicated that their unions had a positive impact on their lives. When asked to describe their spouses the subjects used adjectives such as peaceful, understanding, healing, nurturing, and caring. True modification of one's inner world is not a quick or easy process. Several of the subjects indicated that they experienced difficulties during the initial phases of their marriages. Mrs. Stanford, for example, continues to struggle with the conflict between her current life and her previous expectations. She began crying when describing her husband's attributes. When asked why she replied, "I just feel so grateful. I feel like I'm so lucky. . . . It just feels like I'm not really worthy enough. Like why should I be so lucky." For those individuals who are fortunate enough to grow up in optimal conditions a happy marriage reinforces a positive view of self and other. Many people, of course, are not so fortunate and grow up with treatment that ranges from indifference to abuse. While the results are not generalizable to other populations, for 11 of the current subjects, marriage did provide a welcomed second chance.

It should be understood that insight, change in emotionally significant relationships, and the ameliorating effects of marriage are not mutually exclusive but, in many cases, overlap to some unknown degree. An example of how these factors can contribute to positive change during adult life is exemplified by the life of Herman Crabbe, a subject whose life was examined longitudinally in the Grant Study (Valliant, 1977, pp. 247-248). At 19, Crabbe was viewed as "bizarre" and "suffered perhaps the most pathological mother in the entire Study." His father was crippled and often the target of his wife's paranoid ideation. A social investigator who visited Crabbe's parents wrote "It was the most pathetic interview I've ever had." The evaluation team noted that "Crabbe knew that his mother was clinging to him, but he could not muster the appropriate emotion. Instead he withdrew into the safety of his own head and spent his time with moths not people." He was diagnosed as schizoid. At age 30, Crabbe was described as not seeing people "as they are psychologically but rather in terms of whether or not they provide support, whether they make demands or leave you."

After Herman's mother died both the subject and his father enjoyed a sudden "burst of health" and the father/son relationship improved. One year later Herman's evaluation indicated that he no longer exhibited schizoid symptoms. His "marriage prospered." At age 50, he was evaluated as "a little on the extroverted side." In Crabbe's words he "no longer avoided closeness and familiarity with other people." Instead, he wrote, "I react to events with a good deal of feeling."

To what did Valliant (1977) attribute Crabbe's documented progression away from schizoid fantasy toward meaningful relationships with people?

> First, a danger passed; he was free at last from his mother's psychopathology. Second, at thirty-five, Herman experienced several hours of group psychotherapy. Third, in his early thirties he made friends with his father and for the first time acquired a second parent. Most important, he was blessed with a marriage that was one of the most fulfilling in the Study. He

had married young, and there was no question that in part he married to obtain the competent mother whom he never had. It worked. His wife did far more than college to free him from his family. After twenty-five years of marriage, he could write to the Study, "I have the same wife, and am getting more attached to her all the time." (p. 250)

CONCLUSIONS

This study, like Kotler and Omodei's (1988), Brooks' (1981) and others, offers moderate support for a continuity model to the degree that early attachment relationships appear to have been influential in many of the subjects' lives. The finding that discontinuity might better describe the majority of the subjects' development echoes several of the conclusions that Valiant (1977) reached in the Grant study and those of Egeland, Jacobvitz and Stroufe (1988).

The results from these studies and others also indicated that relationships with others, specifically marital and psychotherapeutic relationships, modified to some extent the deleterious effects of unfortunate childhood experiences. The marital relationship, whether legalized or not, is for the majority of adults, one of life's most important and consequential experiences. Additional research could shed more light on how, for some individuals, it is also the context for emotionally corrective change. Future research should focus on the circumstances in which the marriage relationship is healing.

The findings from this study should provide further encouragement to those members of the therapeutic community who espouse the possibility of characterological change. They particularly support those marriage and family therapists who believe that positive marital and family relationships ameliorate to some degree the childhood developmental immaturities of both spouses and, therefore, pave the way for their children's healthy development (Kirschner and Kirschner, 1986).

Bowlby (1988) believed that therapeutic change occurred when the client was able to use the therapist as a secure base from which to explore the self and his or her interactions in the world. The present results indicate that if troubled spouses can learn from the therapist to provide that resource for one another, the healing process will continue long after the psychotherapy sessions have ended. Each spouse's development or personal growth will enhance the modification of the partner's working model.

The current findings to a large degree confirm the beliefs of Bowlby, Valliant, and others. Tragic events and early vicissitudes did not fully determine the subjects' paths in life. While early interpersonal difficulties can set the stage for later developmental problems, the subjects in this study also found that relationships were healing.

REFERENCES

Ainsworth, M. S. D. (1972). Attachment and dependency: A comparison. In J. L. Gewirtz (Ed.). *Attachment and dependency.* New York: Wiley and Sons.

Ainsworth, M.S.D., & Wittig, B. A. (1969). Attachment and exploratory behavior of one year olds in a strange situation. In B. M. Foss (Ed.), *Determinants of infant behavior* (Vol. 4, pp. 111-136), London: Methuen.

Belsky, J., & Nezworski, T. (1988). *Clinical implications of attachment.* Hillsdale, New Jersey: L. Erlbaum and Associates. (Ed.), *Psychoanalysis and contemporary thought.* (pp. 33-57). London: Hogarth Press.

Bowlby, J. (1973). *Attachment and loss: Vol. 2. Separation: Anxiety and Anger.* New York: Basic.

Bowlby, J. (1979). *The making and breaking of affectional bonds.* London: Tavistock.

Bowlby, J. (1988). *A secure base.* New York: Basic.

Brown, G. W., & Harris, T. (1978). *The social origins of depression.* London: Tavistock.

Brooks, J. (1981). Social maturity in middle-life and its developmental antecedents. In D. Eichorn, J. Clausen, N. Haan, M. Honzik, and P. Muzen (Eds.), *Present and past in middle life.* New York: Academic Press.

Caspi, A., and Elder, G. H. (1987). Emergent family patterns: The intergenerational construction of problem behavior and relationships. In R. A. Hinde and J. Stevenson-Hinde (Eds.), *Relations between relationships.* Oxford: Oxford University Press.

Chess, S., Thomas, A., Korn, S., Mittleman, M., & Cohen, J. (1983). Early parental attitudes, divorce and separation, and young adult outcome: Findings of a longitudinal study. *Journal of the American Academy of Child Psychiatry, 22,* 47-51.

Cohen, L. J. (1974). The operational definition of human attachment. *Psychological Bulletin, 81,* 207-217.

Dunn, J. (1988). Relations among relationships. In S. W. Duck (Ed.), *Handbook of personal relationships.* New York: John Wiley & Sons.

Egeland, B., Jacobvitz, D., & Stroufe, L.A. (1988). Breaking the cycle of abuse. *Child Development, 59,* 1080-1088.

Elder, G. H. (1979). Historical change in life patterns and personality. In P.B. Baltes and O. G. Brim (Eds.), *Lifespan Developments and Behavior, Vol. 2,* New York: Academic Press.

Gove, W., Hughes, M., & Style, C. (1983). Does marriage have positive effects on the psychological well-being of the individual? *Journal of Health and Social Behavior.* (June), 122-131.

Grossman, K., Fremmer-Bombik, E., & Rudolph, J. (1987). Maternal attachment representations as related to child-mother attachment patterns and maternal sensitivity and acceptance of her infant. In R. A. Hinde and J. Stevenson-Hinde (Eds.), *Relations Between Relationships.* Oxford: Oxford University Press.

Jackson, A. (1991). Marriage and attachment: The inner worlds of 10 happily married couples (Doctoral dissertation, University of Pennsylvania, 1991). *Dissertation Abstracts International, 52,* 06A.

Kirschner, D., & Kirschner, S. (1986). *Comprehensive family therapy.*

Kotler, T., & Omodei, M. (1988). Attachment and emotional health: A lifespan approach. *Human relations, 41,* 610-640.

Kotler, T. (1985). Security and autonomy within marriage. *Human Relations, 38*(4), 299-321.

Main, M., & Goldwyn, R. (1984). Predicting rejection of her infant from mother's representation of her own experience: Implications for the abused-abusing intergenerational cycle. *Child Abuse and Neglect, 8,* 203-217.

Main, M., Kaplan, N., & Cassidy, J. (1985). Security in infancy, childhood, and adulthood: A move to the level of representation. In I. Bretherton & E. Walters (Eds.). Growing points of attachment theory and research. *Monographs of the Society for Research in Child Development, 50*(1-2, Serial No. 209), 66-104.

Mattison, S., & Sinclair, I. (1979). *Mate and stalemate.* Oxford: Basil Blackwell.

Morris, D. (1980). *Infant attachment and problem solving in the toddler: Relations to mothers' family history.* Unpublished doctoral dissertation, University of Minnesota.

Morris, D. (1981). Attachment and intimacy. In G. Stricker (Ed.), *Intimacy* (pp. 305-323). New York: Plenum.

Napier, A., & Whitaker, C. (1978). *The family crucible.* New York: Harper & Row.

Ricks, M. (1983). *Individual differences in the preschoolers' competence: Contributions of attachment history and concurrent environmental support.* Unpublished doctoral dissertation, University of Massachusetts-Amherst.

Ricks, M. (1985). The social transmission of parental behavior: attachment across generations. In I. Bretherton & E. Walters (Eds.). Growing points of attachment theory and research. *Monographs of the Society for Research in Child Development, 50* (1-2 Serial No. 209), 211-227.

Rutter, M., & Quinton, D. (1984). Long-term follow-up of women institutionalized in childhood: factors promoting good functioning in adult life. *British Journal of Developmental Psychology, 2,* 191-204.

Valliant, G. (1977). *Adaptation to life.* Boston: Little, Brown and Company.

Objects of Heart's Desire

Bruce J. Schell

SUMMARY. We enter the world with an expectancy of love and a need to love. That which we love is dictated by our histories and limited by our fears. This paper explains some of the consequences of that for the individual and the couple.

We all love someone or something. It may be that our love is ephemeral, arising and fading with the passage of the sun through the sky. It may be that our love is constant, enduring like the stars through the years. The passion of our love may be like a flickering candle or burn with the intensity of a conflagration. Our love may be for a person or power, an idea or beauty, pleasure or physical well being. With some people the presence of their love is obvious. With others its presence is indirectly noted much as the presence of a subterranean river is revealed by the life it makes possible on the surface.

We are all lovers for that is basic to our human nature. The particulars of who or what we love, its intensity, and who or what we feel loved by are shaped by our history. How does our comfort in loving others and our knowledge of ourselves as beloved become lost? How does distrust, anger, and fear blind us to our birthright as lover/beloved? We shall investigate the forces that shape our love

Bruce J. Schell, PhD, is a clinical psychologist and Professor in the Department of Family and Preventive Medicine at the University of South Carolina School of Medicine in Columbia, SC.

[Haworth co-indexing entry note]: "Objects of Heart's Desire," Schell, Bruce J. Co-published simultaneously in the *Journal of Couples Therapy* (The Haworth Press, Inc.) Vol. 4, No. 1/2, 1993, pp. 31-38; and: *Attraction and Attachment: Understanding Styles of Relationships* (ed: Barbara Jo Brothers) The Haworth Press, Inc., 1993, pp. 31-38. Multiple copies of this article/chapter may be purchased from The Haworth Document Delivery Center [1-800-3-HAWORTH; 9:00 a.m. - 5:00 p.m. (EST)].

through an exploration of the consequences when our need to love and to be loved is unsatisfied and then through case examples of couples in psychotherapy. The underlying spirit of this article is expressed in the refrain:

> from you I receive,
> to you I give,
> together we share,
> from this we live.

At the most basic physiological level we are born with an incredible capacity to adapt to different conditions. We are designed, at the genetic level, to survive in widely varying environments. A principle component of this ability to adapt is the relative "plasticity" of our brain function compared to other animals. Much of what we know about the world is based on experience rather than being "hardwired" into the brain. This plasticity allows us to adaptively shape our responses to successfully survive dangerous environments. One of the genetically determined aspects of our brain is that we, for our current age, overassess danger. In a time when physical survival was dependent on remembering and responding to dangerous situations it was vital that once frightened we learned to avoid that danger.

That pro-survival ability continues today to assess danger and shape our avoidance of perceived dangerous situations, but does this predominately in a psychological world and frequently operates unconsciously. Threats to our need for love and to our loving nature are processed along the same brain pathways that once protected us from the saber-toothed tiger. The result is a strong fear reaction to anything that threatens our love and for the conditions surrounding that threat to be highlighted with a mental danger sign. The more threat the developing child received to his/her need for love and to their loving self, the more their internal psychological map is highlighted with danger signs and the more their life is constricted.

The infant is born with a total expectancy of being welcomed and loved. There is no other knowledge than that a love connection is natural. We make precious and rarify that which is perceived as scarce and so have changed our knowledge of the natural place of love in our life into something rare and difficult to obtain. The infant is born in a state of total need and literally does not survive in the absence of those needs being met. Having been born with a total expectancy of and need for their needs to be met, there is a correspondingly total vulnerability. Each failure to meet their needs has an impact on the developing ego and the more severe the deprivation, the more significant the impact on the developing sense of self. The experience of not being received and loved creates deformation of the loving/loved expectancy as well as of the sense of self. This is a deformation of the expectancy and need for love not an elimination of it.

In examining the potential distortions in our lover/beloved sense of self it is of value to think of the self that needs to be loved, the expressions of that need, and the lover that will exactly satisfy the need as a functional unit. Failure to satisfy any aspect of the unit effects the other aspects. For example, if the need is to be loved, the expression of it may be reaching out with arms or lips, and the satisfying lover may be the mother. If the mother is not available, the child will go to the next available person to meet the need. No matter how loving that substitute for the mother is, there will be incomplete satisfaction as it is a substitute for the mother, not the mother. If the need is repeatedly unmet at the human level, the child will seek satisfaction with non-human objects. With continued frustration, awareness of the need and its original satisfying object are submerged and satisfaction is sought with a new substituted object. Over time, with repeated partial satisfaction the child begins to identify the need as related to the substituted object. If, for example, food was the partial solution to the need to be loved then when the loving impulse arises it would be experienced as a need for food. No matter how sated with food, since the need was for love, there remains a sense of being unfulfilled, that something is missing.

Linus and his blanket, from the Charlie Brown cartoons, provides a good visual example of the need satisfaction expressed with a non-human object, the blanket. Linus is always seen with the blanket, which illustrates a consequence of the substitute love object not being the original satisfying object. Incomplete satisfaction of the need increases the attachment to the object which is expressed in a compulsive relationship with it. So we could consider the blanket for Linus as his solution to the absence of, for example, an available mothering one and/or excessive fear attached to meeting that need with humans.

The need for love and intimacy continues as a central organizing principle of life, but its expression grows increasingly obscure as the failure to satisfy the need is repeated. What we have learned about the nature of love and ourself in relationship to love is an important determinant of our personality structure. Our strategies to obtain love, our beliefs concerning love and concerning ourself as a love object, and our beliefs regarding the relative scarcity or abundance of love, all are reflected in our personality structure.

An evolving part of my practice is to spend some time examining what people believe about themselves as lovers and as the object of someone else's love. Some have a very clear vision of themselves as a lover, but their image of themselves as someone's beloved is missing except, as it is reflected in their view of themselves as a lover. It is as if they believe that the pleasure of their beloved is as close as they can get to being loved. Others easily see themselves as loved in their immaturity but cannot imagine themselves loved in their maturity. So we explore what the person has learned about the relative abundance or scarcity of love, their strategies to obtain love, how those strategies differ between men and women, and what occurs when love is available.

There are a multitude of strategies to try to ensure that love or intimacy will occur. Some common ones are to become the cute child, the controlling one, the loving child, the angry one, the frightened vulnerable child, the worried one, the hardworking, brave, and self-sacrificial child. Each of our strategies, as lovers and beloved are our strengths and failings in the couple relationship.

An aspect of treatment in psychotherapy involves distinguishing between the absence of love and when so much of the love/beloved energy is bound to nonhuman sources of satisfaction that little of the person remains available to either love or be loved. Repeated partial satisfaction through nonhuman objects binds a certain portion of our love energy to that object. With that binding and the others that take place, over time, under ordinary circumstances there is progressively less available for human relationships.

In the first flush of love the importance of the nonhuman love objects is temporarily decreased. In a sense, the range and depth of our possibilities as lover/beloved are revealed during this time. With the waning of that first flush of love the person's availability to love and be loved may diminish. When that diminishment leads to the couple presenting for psychotherapy, it is valuable to explore how much of their capacity to love and be loved is bound to other people and to nonhuman objects. There can be significant relief in their discovering that they or their partner was not born with a deficiency in the ability to love, but rather it is bound to other sources of satisfaction. We begin to examine the various objects their love is bound to and the conditions surrounding how those objects became a solution to their need to love and to be loved. I am not positing that all nonhuman passionate involvements represent displacement of unmet early needs. Signs that suggest that possibility are addictive features in relationship to the object. This may include anxiety at the possibility of not interacting with the object, a compulsive quality to the interaction with it, and the timing of the use of it suggesting a primary mood altering purpose.

The following case study highlights features of the binding process and the consequences within a couple.

Harry is a 40 year old once divorced man who is married to Judy, a 34 year old woman who had been in several very important relationships. They had been married approximately two years when they entered psychotherapy. They had a premarital relationship of approximately one year, but had not lived together. They each described feeling in love with and loved by the other during their courtship and during the early months of their marriage.

They entered psychotherapy at her insistence. She had grown concerned over the waning of her feelings of being loved and how he seemed less emotionally available to her love. He felt their relationship was satisfactory, even though he conceded the intensity of their contact had diminished. He saw that as a normal consequence of the marital relationship and used his previous marriage as proof of that. His parents had divorced when he was young, and he had been primarily raised by his mother who was an explosive alcoholic. He described memories of his mother threatening him with a pistol, threatening to shoot him if he misbehaved. Judy's history, by comparison, was much more benign with clear memories of her parents loving relationship and of feeling cared for by both parents. However, in elaborating on this she described her father as busy and frequently unavailable.

In exploring with Harry where he felt safe, loved, and cared for, the predominate area was in music. He described how in conflictful or frightening situations he would turn to music and quickly feel soothed and removed from those situations. He currently has an extensive collection of CD's, which hold a place of honor in their home. In his life the most constant and reliable relationship was with music. Judy observed that many of their evenings were spent with him listening to music. When he played his guitar he would isolate himself and become angry if she entered the room.

We love when we feel safe and with whom (what) we feel safe. The two issues facing Harry were how to feel safe with Judy and how to free some of the love energy bound to music and therefore unavailable to his relationship. A frequent issue at this point is that while the person's actions are controlled by their fear, they are unaware of it. In part that arises from our tendency to block awareness of fear with another effect. Boredom, indifference and anger are frequent blocking affects.

In the safety of the psychotherapy hour it is possible for the patient to free some of the bound love energy and bring it to the couple relationship. We first explored the meaning of music at the cognitive and emotional level. The approach was patterned after Pesso (1973). That approach emphasizes that we are symbol-making and symbol-using beings and that it is possible to modify important psychological structures through the use of a person's symbol system. The most effective way of doing this is to make literal and tangible the meaning of their symbols. For this to occur there must be a safe enough atmosphere for people to re-enter and re-experience their vulnerability and the wounding of that vulnerability.

With the creation of a safe enough atmosphere Harry was able to invest some of the sense of safety and love that was bound to music in consciously created symbolic figures. The symbolic figures were people or objects that he chose to enact aspects of his internal conflicts and aspects of his symbolic solution to these conflicts. We might think of this as a conscious creation and utilization of a "transitional object." A transitional object whose function is to free energy bound to his historical (music) solution and make it available to his current relationship. The steps involved were those required to remain true to his internal reality and to his sense of personal safety. The effect was for him to discover more of a sense of possibility in the world, to feel safer, and to have an increased capacity to love and be loved in his relationship to Judy.

We have looked at one consequence of a person's early environment forcing a substitute solution to the love need. That solution left Harry present but removed love from the relationship. In the next case we shall examine, the love remains but in an essential way the person is removed from the relationship. It is arguable that unless you are fully present the love expressed, is at least partially false. Durang (1985) in *The Marriage of Bette and Boo* expressed it this way;

> Unless you go through all the genuine anguish that you feel, both justified and unjustified, the feeling of love that you do have will not have any legitimate base and will be at least partially false. Plus, eventually you will go crazy.

In general, to love the other and to express it requires a trust that our love will be accepted. Where there is excessive concern over its reception we become timid in its expression and vigilant concerning its reception. For intimacy and love to be present and experienced between two people, two selves must be present. If one or both people are overly focused on how they are received then there is a tendency to lose track of the self in focusing on the other's reaction. This eventuates in the other becoming a judge of our love, resulting in an exchange between a superior and an inferior.

Our primary information about the expression of love is the way we and our intimates were treated. Helen, 38, and Luke, 39, have been married for 20 years. They entered psychotherapy after she read some of the adult children of alcoholic's material. Helen came from a home in which her father was a frequently absent alcoholic and her mother was very controlling and deprecating of her. Luke's father was a religious fanatic and an absolute ruler of his wife and children. His mother was warm, loving, submissive to his father, and died when he was 16.

They both learned, in the name of love, to vigilantly watch the other. She watched in the hope of pleasing and thereby earning his love. He watched in the hope that if he controlled enough he would never be left. The development of their full selves in relationship to each other had been neglected in their fearful preoccupation with each other. As she began to focus more of her awareness on herself, she began to grieve for her neglected self and then to rage against a lifetime of being controlled. His focus on himself thrust him back to his mother's death and his continued fear of abandonment. Amidst the sparks generated by these two growing selves an occasional flash of love is seen. They continue in psychotherapy.

Underneath the surface storms that couples bring to psychotherapy, there remains the powerful current of their love. If we, as psychotherapists, focus on handling the storm and lose awareness of the deeper currents, we risk perpetuating their early less than optimal solutions to their need to love and be loved. It is vital to remember that often we are treating the parents of the next generation. If, in our work we help them more completely live the full range of their loving nature then the birthright of their children will be enriched.

Appraisal of the couple's beliefs about themselves as lovers and as beloved furthers the shift from the myopic view that their immediate distress produces, to one that supports the process of becoming more fully human. That is, it becomes possible for them to see their current distress in the context of their total history and of their potential future possibilities.

In a previous article (Schell, 1992) I suggested the importance of an appraisal of the couples spiritual life. In this article I emphasized an appraisal of the couples' beliefs concerning love. As psychotherapists it is our vision of the couples' possibilities that deeply influence the process, content, and outcome of our work with them. What we attend to and what we neglect help shape the immediate outcome of psychotherapy, and for many couples, the long term outcome of their lives.

REFERENCES

Durang, C. (1985). *The marriage of Bette and Boo*. New York: Dramatist Play Service Inc.

Pesso, A. (1973). *Experience in action*. New York: New York University Press.

Schell, B. (1992. Elements of couple psychotherapy and awakening. *Journal of Couples Therapy*, 3(1).

Response to Bruce J. Schell's Article: "Objects of Heart's Desire"

Loving is the purpose of life. One is born being pure love rather than learning love; the rejection of this love creates a lifelong striving to reattain the state of loving bliss–loving for the joy and awe of loving. B. Schell's description of love development with its distortions is excellent although I believe the infant has only love to give and the learning process is how to have it received rather than how to obtain it. The same distortions occur in either event. I do disagree with his idea that one loves power, beauty, pleasure, etc.

Love is the natural human state. Beauty and ideas may touch a person deeply to open up the innate love within. One appreciates beauty which releases the loving energy, rather than loving beauty. Many positive experiences and emotions may unlock one's capacity for love and thus begin the path of achieving the purpose of life.

The drive for power is the result of an absence of love. It is an ego distortion with the purpose being to obtain love, not to love. Melanie Klein (*Envy and Gratitude,* 1965) describes greed as the fear that one will not obtain sufficient love, so one tries to get as much as possible before it is withdrawn. This, as an adult ego, is so insecure that it believes power will convince others to love it. We are loved for being, not for achieving. The latter is a distortion of love resulting in the oxymoron of "conditional love." Envy, greed and jealousy are derived from the concept of scarcity–that there will

[Haworth co-indexing entry note]: "Response to Bruce J. Schell's Article: "Objects of Heart's Desire," Alexana, Aliya. Co-published simultaneously in the *Journal of Couples Therapy* (The Haworth Press, Inc.) Vol. 4, No. 1/2, 1993, pp. 39-40; and: *Attraction and Attachment: Understanding Styles of Relationships* (ed: Barbara Jo Brothers) The Haworth Press, Inc., 1993, pp. 39-40. Multiple copies of this article/chapter may be purchased from The Haworth Document Delivery Center [1-800-3-HAWORTH; 9:00 a.m. - 5:00 p.m. (EST)].

not be enough love. All other scarcities are substitutes for insuffi-
cient love.

Unfortunately a major factor of the human condition is that one's
capacity for loving is cut off from awareness and expression
through fear and the pain of life. I agree with Schell that we respond
to emotional fears with a primal reality, but emotional losses are
more confusing and stressful to a developing ego than the direct
fear of a known physical threat. All fear is the direct or indirect
anxiety of the loss of love. The fear in turn causes insecurity, doubt,
mistrust, hopelessness, pain, resentment, anguish and despair.
Transformation of the fear into pure love and acceptance is necessary to begin loving. This is the purpose of the therapy process.
People seek love from others and believe in error that their appreciation of being loved is actual loving. It is true that various types of
appreciation and gratitude can open the heart to experience true
loving of other.

We seek human love in an effort to tap the love energy locked
within us. In fact, most relationships become so bound with expectations that true loving is not achieved–the primal fear of loss while
risking intimacy interfering with that possibility. If the relationship
can achieve enough security, one can succeed in opening the channel
of love from within and the experience of loving another can begin.
As this loving expands, one gradually experiences divine as well as
human love. Increased divine love increases human love in turn. This
process continues until one attains again the capacity for pure loving
that was lost at birth. Allowing oneself to know such loving and love
(lover and beloved–Schell) enables a communion with man and God
that fills the soul with awe and joy–the natural state of being.

Sexual Intimacy–
Towards Equal Relationships
Between Men and Women
(with Treatment Assistance
of a Computer Program)

Louis Sommeling

SUMMARY. By rethinking sexual basic concepts we liberate sexology from mere biological and technical models. The sexual focus combined with the Object Relation Theory creates a promising therapeutic perspective for couples. Special attention will be given to male processes. Some vignettes of the computer program Sexpertise illustrate this article.

In our days the equal relationship between men and women is a difficult one. In this article we will rethink some of the sexual rituals between men and women, specifically such basic concepts as arousal, desire and also some power-aspects as they can occur in a sexual relationship.

Further down we will discuss the implicit philosophies of thera-

Louis Sommeling, PhD Psychologist, is a psychotherapist at the Groningen University in Holland and Sexologist at the Rutgers Foundation (Dutch National Institute for treatment of sexual problems), is Fellow of the Dutch Group Psychotherapy Association and the International Pesso Psychotherapy Federation. At present he is working on a book about Male Desire.

[Haworth co-indexing entry note]: "Sexual Intimacy–Towards Equal Relationships Between Men and Women (with Treatment Assistance of a Computer Program)," Sommeling, Louis. Co-published simultaneously in the *Journal of Couples Therapy* (The Haworth Press, Inc.) Vol. 4, No. 1/2, 1993, pp. 41-59; and: *Attraction and Attachment: Understanding Styles of Relationships* (ed: Barbara Jo Brothers) The Haworth Press, Inc., 1993, pp. 41-59. Multiple copies of this article/chapter may be purchased from The Haworth Document Delivery Center [1-800-3-HAWORTH; 9:00 a.m. - 5:00 p.m. (EST)].

pists, which still remain sometimes unconscious. This would influence treatment options and their effectiveness.

Rethinking a sexual focus, combined with the Object Relation Theory, supplies a clear paradigm for better understanding of both the female and the male partners. Special attention will be given to the understanding of the resistance of men in therapeutic processes. The issue of gender from the male perspective in relation to psychotherapy is until today not very well developed in the international therapeutic community.[1]

Surprisingly, the computer can aid the treatment of sexual intimacy problems without necessarily disturbing the therapeutic encounter. The Sexpertise programs as developed and spoken of here, will assist therapists as well as clients in making some expertise and experience concrete and available. This expertise has been developed mainly by the Rutgers Foundation, the Dutch National Institute for treatment of current sexual problems. (In the Low Countries, initially research was focused on problems resulting from a restrictive sexual morality. During the 1970s attention shifted to the rapid process of sexual liberalization and its practical consequences, such as the need for family planning education and services. The past decade was largely dominated by two issues: sexual abuse, including possible sexual contacts between helpers and clients, and research on sexually transmitted diseases. As most of these studies have been published in the Dutch language only, they have not sufficiently added to the international body of knowledge. This is regrettable because, particularly the Netherlands is now characterized by an open and permissive attitude regarding sexuality, which gives it quite a unique position in the world, not just in terms of attitudes and behavior, but also in terms of research possibilities.)

TOWARDS A PSYCHOLOGY OF HUMAN SEXUALITY

Today, modern sexologists agree that sexuality is first and foremost a psychological reality. Contrary to previous thoughts, our sexual behavior is not totally guided by a biological drive, but comes as a combination of hormones and humanly learned experience as well as its interpretation. These three factors together shape the characteristics of human sexuality. To say it in a popular way: sex is not only between our legs, but also between our ears!

In aiding our clients as therapists, we should help to become explicit about sexual arousal as well as the hidden needs we human beings are longing for. Also, some attention to the power aspects of the sexual game may support clients in shaping their personal sexual life.

Rethinking Sexual Arousal

The *arousal curve of* the American researchers Masters and Johnson (1966) has been given much publicity. It showed what happened following effective stimulation of penis and clitoris. This model of Masters and Johnson suggests, briefly, that partners must pass through this whole curve at all times, in order for them to have 'healthy' sex. Actually the effect of this model in practice may be called rather dubious: as if this ought to be everybody's *"natural"* reaction, as if one ought to reach this norm in order to be classified as 'normal and healthy' beings. In our daily practice however, if you ask people to draw their arousal curve, this "standard curve" seldomly emerges. Rather, you'll see flat and steep lines, long take-off runs, nice detours, etc. (Figure 1).

Helen Kaplan (1974) describes how, in its suggestive clarity, the curve of Masters and Johnson turns out to be a simplification of reality: there is no such thing as a continuously rising process. In physical arousal there are two stages to be distinguished:

a. a genital-vagocongestive reaction (mainly blood supply, resulting in erection, moistening of the vagina and swelling of the labia)
b. a reflexive reaction of the flesh (primarily muscular, resulting in contraction of the muscles and orgasm).

So, partners, experiencing sexuality, embark on a sort of a two-stage rocket: a continuous stimulation of one stage could ignite the other. The value of Kaplan's findings is the insight that one stage being ignited, does not necessarily imply that the other stage has to be turned on too.

FIGURE 1. The computer program Personal Sexpertise provides couples with help in dealing with sexual intimacy. X has noted the average excitement course of her/his partner. The partner gives an opinion of X's notations.

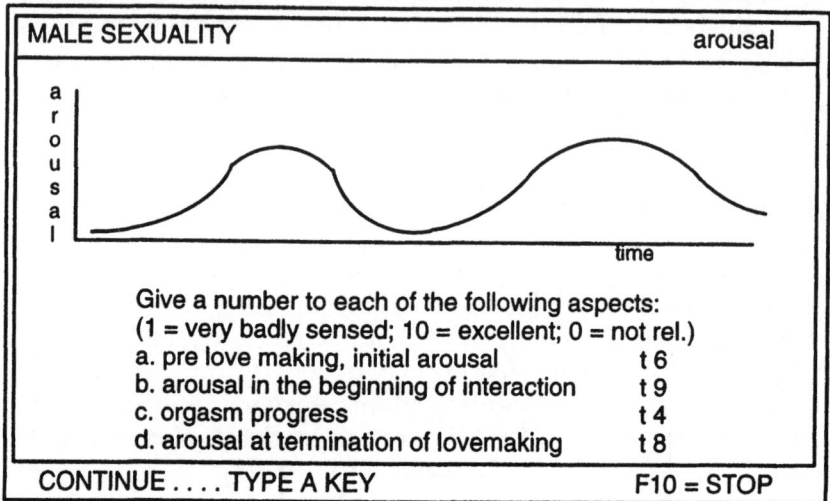

```
┌─────────────────────────────────────────────────────────────┐
│ MALE SEXUALITY                                        arousal │
│                                                               │
│  a                                                            │
│  r                                                            │
│  o                                                            │
│  u                                                            │
│  s                                                            │
│  a                                                            │
│  l └──────────────────────────────────────────────           │
│                                                  time         │
│                                                               │
│       Give a number to each of the following aspects:        │
│       (1 = very badly sensed; 10 = excellent; 0 = not rel.)   │
│       a. pre love making, initial arousal          t 6        │
│       b. arousal in the beginning of interaction   t 9        │
│       c. orgasm progress                           t 4        │
│       d. arousal at termination of lovemaking      t 8        │
├─────────────────────────────────────────────────────────────┤
│ CONTINUE . . . . TYPE A KEY                        F10 = STOP │
└─────────────────────────────────────────────────────────────┘
```

Here is how this has been conveyed to clients in the Personal Sexpertise program. In a mini-lecture on the arousal curve, (submenu for men), the following text appears on the screen:

Arousal does not necessarily have to end in orgasm. If arousal is like a walk up a mountain, then people can also stop halfway for a 'nice picnic on a mountain meadow.' After this, they may return to the valley, or go for the top anyway. So you have more than one way of making love at your disposal. The chosen way will probably fit much better your own wishes and possibilities as a woman or as a man. There is more than penis-centered top-excitement. Using sex this way, men will widen their possibilities of arousal. As a baby, a men's skin was a sensual organ from top to bottom, not just his penis. Later on in puberty boys would feel aroused by a single glance, a manner of walking, a nice figure, a looking forward to a meeting. This wide scale of erotic experiences often fades away for men, and that's too bad. It can be regained, though, for sexuality is not only made up by physically conditioned processes, but above all by ideas we've been talked into in the years that we've been living.

The fact that not only the clients but also many professionals still tend to think in terms of a merely biological model of sexuality too, has far-reaching consequences. To name some examples: unnecessary medical operations are still performed (e.g., for vaginism or a tight foreskin). Mythical prejudices are perpetuated, e.g., about asexuality of older women and men. Also, there are many no-sense making intake questions for clients, such as: "How many times do you do it?" There are more important questions to be asked than, e.g., the latter, as we will see in the next section.

Sexual Desire: What Are We Looking for in Sex?

Object Relation theorists state that libido is object-seeking and not primarily pleasure-seeking. Our needs are deeply psychological and not merely biologically rooted. Sometimes in sexual desire people want to touch mythical depths. At other times they want to fulfill a more basic human need, such as there are: support, nurturance, protection and "limitation"[2] (Pesso, 1992). We can, in some ways of kissing someone else, basically seek the fulfillment of our own need for nurturance. In caressing along our body-contours, our identity and ego-boundaries are tenderly limited and validated. Holding one another in the darkness of the blankets, we protect and/or find protection. There are many 'erogenic' zones in the body as places where we can get–not strictly sexual–support (e.g., behind the knees, the small of the back, the buttocks).

In an amusing story Lillian Rubin[3] gives an illustration of how this can work with mainly not so much biological, but more psychological components of our so called 'sexual' excitements. She interviewed a man who felt very excited when he "got" a women into orally stimulating him; he felt an extreme power over her submissiveness. Then Rubin interviewed his female partner: she felt herself aroused by the same act of fellatio: she experienced power over the extreme vulnerability of the man!

In his investigations Fisher (1973) found at least eighty reasons for people to want to have sex. (For a categorization and therapeutic applications see Figure 2).

FIGURE 2. Screen of Personal Sexpertise: support in explicating implicit expectations of couples on desire. X has asked himself what his partner expects from sex. The partner gives an opinion as to the correctness of X's rotation.

```
┌──────────────────────────────────────────────────────────────────────┐
│ MALE SEXUALITY                                            WHY SEX?     │
├──────────────────────────────────────────────────────────────────────┤
│ F1=  ACKNOWLEDGMENT AND STATUS (test to discover whether or not you're │
│      important enough for the other to be interested)                  │
│ F2=  PROTECTION AND DEPENDENCY (securely hidden away, seeking or giving │
│      protection)                                                       │
│ F3=  FEELINGS OF POWER (testing if you can influence circumstances the way you │
│      want, taking possession of the other).                           │
│ F4=  LOVE, AFFECTION (wanting to feel that the other appreciates you in all aspects │
│      and v.v.)                                                         │
│ F5=  PHYSICALLY WELLBEING (experience of lust, content, release of tension) │
│ F6=  INDEPENDENCE (keeping your reserve, being above sexual dependency, │
│      sexualize intimate feelings)                                      │
│ F7=  THERE IS NOT ONE THING THAT ALWAYS TAKE PREVALENCE (it changes)   │
│ F8=  ANYTHING ELSE, NOT MENTIONED HERE                                 │
│ F9=  HE DOESN'T KNOW                                                   │
│      -----------------------------                                     │
│ Harry chose for you: F1                                                │
│                                                                        │
│                                                                        │
│ TYPE A FUNCTION KEY:                                     F10 = STOP    │
└──────────────────────────────────────────────────────────────────────┘
```

What are we looking for in sex? When people come with sex problems it is important for therapists to invite them to think about their needs by asking such a question. But giving an answer to this question would suggest that people have an awareness of why they want something. Most of the time however, unconscious needs play a role in the background.

If we ask a client 'What is it you are looking for in sex, why do you do it?', the obvious answer is usually something like: 'Because I love it.' If you keep on asking however, often there turns out to be a good deal more to it. Possible hidden motivations could be: 'to relieve my sexual tension,' 'to make another person feel nice and comfortable,' 'to prevent a fight at home,' 'otherwise I wouldn't live up to the standard coitus frequency of the average man and that makes me feel sure,' etc. People tend to sexualize their human needs. In those cases, they may use an 'improper' way to express those needs. They would have been better served, had they been able to express this some other way.

Inviting clients to think about their sexual motivations will supply alternatives. It creates possibilities to act in a more adequate and personal way and to better meet our needs. Especially male therapists (Aghassy, 1984, 1990) can sometimes make mistakes in the interpretation of the behavior of their clients: behavior which looks on the surface 'sexual' can often also be interpreted as testing behavior or as a need for approval, support or affection.

Power-Aspects of Rules, Definitions and Therapy-Strategies

Belief systems, rooted in secret sex-specific ideas, sometimes have hidden power in our world. In the section above, we eluded to a different paradigm from the biologically oriented definitions of sexuality as they have emerged in a male oriented society.

Now, in the next paragraphs, we will look more closely to the influence this has had on clients and on therapists.

Sex can be seen as a game with rules (Vennix, 1981). Discussing the rules can open couples' eyes for the power aspects of their sexual encounters. The definitions of the rules may seem "natural," but who has written them? It may be helpful in a therapeutic approach, to aid clients in re-owning their own, individually appropriated rules.

> The computer program Personal Sexpertise helps to open client's eyes for gender-specifically formulated rules.
>
> Here is an example of a male rule: 'The penis is the organ which offers the most pleasure, so a nicely fitting vagina is the best thing you can have.'
>
> If women were to formulate these rules in a similar way, how would this same rule be reformulated in this case? [In the computer program the user is enabled to formulate her or his own answer to these questions.]
>
> In this case such could be: 'The clitoris is the organ which offers the most pleasure, so soft fingers or a nice, able tongue is what one should look for in a man.'
>
> A second example of a male rule: 'For me intercourse ends in a lovely orgasm; if she has her pleasure too, that's a wel-

come bonus.' In reverse the female rule can be: 'As a rule I don't climax during intercourse. I do, if we pet to climax; if he comes too while petting, good for him.'

Therapists should be conscious of the influence their own gender-specific ideas can have on the therapeutic treatments they offer. In the daily practice of a Dutch sexologist for example, one can often encounter the following scene:

> The couple comes in and he may say: "She never feels like it."
> She nods "yes" and feels guilty.
> He points at her and thinks: "She is the patient."

Which paradigm will lead the therapist here in his/her interpretations? The paradigms in the strategy we offer will have far reaching consequences for treatment![4]

In the computer program Sexpertise Professional, the program which accompanies the Personal Sexpertise, some choices and their consequences are listed:

As a therapist, you may think:

1. "Most likely there's something wrong with her. For that reason she'll need a psychological or physical examination."
2. "We'll start a therapy to teach her to own her sexual feelings, for that's what she lacks."
3. "We'll try and teach him how to lessen his libido."
4. "We don't speak about sexuality at all, because our focus is on relationship problems; relationship problems are always "deeper" than sexual problems."
5. "We are going to talk about their different expectations and belief systems regarding sex . . ."

Option 1 and 2 are typically macho points of view: the engine has broken down and must be repaired. She is being labeled as the patient. Therapy based on such assumptions, is likely to fail (the covered aggression, showing itself in the body resistance, is not explored). Medical examinations are here performed unnecessarily. Medical treatment is only indicated in the case of physical pain or use of medicine. In most cases there is nothing wrong with the body. That there should be something wrong in a psychiatric sense with the woman is also not the first option in this common case.

Option 2: It is not clear why she doesn't feel like having sex. The problem 'lack of libido' mostly has its cause elsewhere. Maybe he is the one who is a poor lover, who has no notion of her form of sexuality. And she may not be aware either of the fact that she may have her own, different from his, forms of erotic desire.

Often, in therapeutic interventions, a choice is made here for one of the two partners. And often this choice is in favor of the man's view and against the woman's. (It is assumed that she's the one who needs to change.) That is why such a therapeutic intervention is bound to end in failure.

Men will usually say: when sex is okay, the relation will be okay. In reverse women will often say: when the relation is okay, sex will be okay. True, she may, also in this case, turn out to be the one who has an obvious problem, e.g., she can't have an orgasm, even while she herself would very much like to have one. Or she may be so tensed up that a penis cannot enter her (vaginismus) and she as well as he, would like to change that. This need to change does not need to be only for the relationship, but could also be really for herself. In that case a therapy for her would be indicated. But frequently it is the man too, who has some sort of trouble.

> Comparable to vaginismus with a woman, a man can suffer from a tight foreskin; this can also be because he is afraid of sex, or has never learned to masturbate properly. In such a situation, that should also be paid attention to. But not primarily by the doctor: a psychotherapist can provide him with some exercises to widen the foreskin and overcome anxiety.

Option 3: It may be an original and radically feministic option to point towards the male partner as the one who must change. The question is, however, will it become clear this way why she has not been able to solve her part of their problem without therapy? In this option the man is being labeled as the patient: the therapist sides too much in that case with the woman. For that reason this type of treatment is also likely to fail.

Option 4: Couples therapists in general tend to perceive sexuality as a "deeper," i.e., a communicative problem. If they do so, they will not talk explicitly about sexuality. Such an attitude, however, can also be a rationalization of the therapist's own inhibitions. Many clients, coming to our institute after analytic or mere communication therapy, complain that, because of their experiencing their problems as sexual, their therapist's attitude is not compatible. Would it not show mere respect for a therapist to enter the intervention through the client's entrance (and perhaps exit by one's own)?[5]

Option 5: In my opinion the choice to talk first about the different expectations and ideas about sex with the client is the most appropriate. It could be, that the woman does not feel like having sex, because she has no choice but sit at home all day long, while he is out there in the world. Or there may be something else she hates. After all this has been explored and she turns out to be interested in doing something about sex, the problem may be defined as follows: Perhaps sex to them is only having intercourse and it is just that which the woman does not like (but has not dared to speak out about it so far).

So *before starting* any kind of sex therapy there are other things we have to do as therapists. First, it has to become clear that a woman has a right to her own kind of erotic life and this can be different from his wishes. In the same way, we may have to convince the man that there is more to sex than penis-centered arousal.[6] Furthermore we may have to show that sex therapy is not just a question of labeling one partner as *the* patient.

Generally the difficulty is to be found *between* partners; so they both have to take their responsibilities. But first of all we have to talk about their different expectations and ideas about sex. Having discussed these topics, the ground is prepared for training new behavior and new forms of making love (and now the body- and skin-focusing aspects of the Masters and Johnson exercises may be a useful approach).

MALE SEXUALITY AND OBJECT RELATION THEORY

The sexual focus as elaborated upon and rethought in the first section of this article, now will be integrated and completed with a perspective which relates to the Object Relation Theory. These two approaches put together, illuminate a paradigm which can guide our therapeutic interventions.

My research shows that group or communication therapy for couples mostly effects women, in the sense that they become more assertive; men only feel a little more connected, but in general do not experience real individual change (Sommeling, 1991). This article will end by describing our experience with this *dual therapeutic focus* as a promising perspective especially for men to change their behavior.

Desire and Autonomy

The bridge between the two approaches was built by Winnicot. He formulated the relationship between healthy autonomy and adult sexual arousal management:

> Being able to enjoy being alone with another person who is alone, is in itself an experience of health. Lack of id-tension may produce anxiety but time-integration of the personality enables the individual to wait for the natural return of id-tension ... (Winnicot, 1965)

This then leads us to asking an interesting question about sexuality: "Do we seek contact with another person because we are aroused?" or "Do we long for someone and therefore make ourselves excited?" (Schmidt, 1974). Sometimes we have to stand by, *wait* and sustain, without getting anxious.

To me it came as a shock when someone asked me for the first time, (referring to the Masters and Johnson curve): "Which part is the interactive phase, and which part the solophase?" The initial stage of love making is highly interactive, there is a lot of contact with the partner and arousal can arise here by stimulating each other. But the middle part in which intercourse and orgasm has its place, is adequately named the *solo*phase.[7] Especially during this latter phase partners will be more on their own and solo. Despite all the romantic illusions about 'togetherness' we can only experience a true orgasm, if we decide to shift our focus of attention away from our partner and more to ourselves, from interaction to individual experience.

(The stereotyped ideal and norm of "having an orgasm together" only can mean that both individuals have an orgasm at the same time). By accepting there is always "something between," by realizing our existential aloneness and individuality, we grow toward becoming autonomous partners. The so-called "primary sexual problems"[8] then, rooted in the individual case-history, primarily are to be found in this solophase-area. And the so called "secondary problems" mostly have to do with a lack of sufficient interactive skills (Everaerd, 1981). Today *sexual problems with intimacy in men are not, generally speaking, caused by a lack of interactive skills but are primarily rooted in their individual case-history.* So in therapy we have to focus on individuation–separation processes too and guide men to develop true autonomy. Psychologists like Nancy Choderow et al. have described the problematic character of male identity (based in the dilemma of not being the mother and not being able to find a figure of identification in a psychologically absent father). We as men have learned that separation is more real than intimate connection. We are individuated but have not grown to autonomy.[9] We often experience fear of symbiotic engulfment and defend ourselves by drawing our boundaries well by withdrawal and by controlling the other person involved. While deeply longing for connection with the other, we confuse at the same time "contact" with "symbiosis," by reactively wanting to claim and to possess women. We throw a "temper tantrum" if we don't get what we so desperately want. Therefore also in sexual relationship true contact is only possible after disentanglement from individual symbiotic illusions and after finding the "optimal distance."

Couples Therapy and Processes of Men

In ten years of group therapy with couples who have sexual desire problems, at first we, the therapists, mainly saw changes in women, but no real individual changes in men. In later years, men also experienced larger changes (Sommeling, 1991).

What was the secret of this shifting with the increase of the treatment effects? First of all I was having a relationship with a self confident woman and in my own therapy process was focussing on personal change. But also I had a good working relationship with the female co-therapist; so we became a better identification-model for the couples we worked with.

Secondly, we managed and developed a *dual* focus of therapeutic interventions. Next to exploring the cognitions about sex as mentioned above, our interventions were more analytically focused on individuation-separation aspects.

By describing Group Focal Conflicts[10] according to Whitaker and Lieberman (1964) we discovered successive phases in the changes the men went through and in the way they were working through their inner processes.

These phases were:

a. *Stage of anxious entanglement.* In the beginning of group-therapy, couples sit next to each other and speak about themselves in terms of "we."

b. *Stage of aggression and accusation in terms of "she" and "he."* Men and women are no longer sitting next to each other. The men accuse their wives of not wanting sex, and advise them to go see a doctor or the sex therapist. With this statement men take the one-up position of "sitting in a waiting-room," but at the same time keeping themselves in the submissive position of letting go of the solution of the problem! Here, we get a glimpse of the profound depths of some of men's problematic feelings towards women (often rooted in negative mother projections); they can "eat" the mother, they have "rights" because they are married and therefore the "owners" of the female body.

c. *Stage of distance, the massive "no" of the women.* Women have in this stage developed solidarity with each other, have grown assertive and self-confident. This leads to more confusion in the men and they started to feel more scared. "Blaming my partner" doesn't seem to work anymore in this stage of the group therapy for couples.

d. *The final stage: transition from individuation to autonomy.* The therapists' support is especially needed for men in this anxiety causing stage. The male part of the clients begin to speak in terms of "feeling" and in the "I-form": "I, as a man, felt depressed, isolated, abandoned and not loved." Such a state of confusion turned out to be the painful condition for the development of more autonomy. Now is the time for the men to slowly start identifying with the (encouraging) male therapist and with the other men in the room, the famous "male bond" (Tripp, 1976).

Masculine Spirituality

The difficulty which men co-experience in staying alone for sometime without looking outside themselves for another symbiotic confusion, is beautifully pictured in Nelson's lecture *Male Sexuality and Masculine Spirituality (1991)*:

> Women tend to experience their sexuality as internal, deep and mysterious. As a male on the other hand, I am often inclined to experience my sexuality as more instrumental. My penis is an instrument for penetrating and exploring a mystery which is essentially external to me. And the linearity, the hardness, the straightness of the prized erection all are important to my understanding of reality. Then spiritually (. . .) I am prone to believe that mystery is "out there" rather than sensing the mystery dwelling within me (. . . .).
>
> The flaccid penis is empty of the engorging blood which brings hard excitement to the phallus. Flaccidity is letting go of all urgency; the spiritual experience of sinking, letting go and emptying is an experience of divine grace, as interpreted in the Christian tradition. It means trusting God that we do not need to *do*, that our *being* is enough. It means trusting ourselves to the darkness. . . .

I would like to conclude here that autonomy is a condition for real sexual intimacy. It seems that especially men have to learn to be alone (which is something essentially different from withdrawal!). Instead of waiting until the woman will love him, a man has to learn the secret that only in a position of true autonomy is he able to be attractive. In that position of autonomy a man can take at the same time responsibility for the sexual and the communicative problems he and his partner are having as a couple. In such a position he will be less emotionally dependent on his partner and consequently claim her less as well.

When one of the male sex symbols of the eighties, William Hurt, won an Oscar, I asked some female clients what made him so attractive to them. Here are some of their answers: "He looks at you, really seeing you too, and at the same time he is true to himself."–"He is his own; he gives a lot, yet does not drown in it." In an interview Hurt himself said: "I think I discovered a long time ago, and rediscovered sometimes, that I am alone–not that I'm lonely, but I am alone."

Only autonomous partners are capable of having a good relationship and a human sexuality which is satisfying to both. The dual focus, as described above, of rethought sexual basic concepts and of attention for autonomy creates a clear paradigm for men to understand themselves.

WITH A LITTLE HELP OF THE COMPUTER

This article is illustrated with some computer vignettes. Therapists tend to look down on computers, but clients are enthusiastic (Schwartz, 1984). Schwartz studied the use of computers in clinical practice and even mentions transference feelings. Binik (1988) and Reitman (1984) describe the use of computers in self help sex-therapy for some restricted sexual dysfunctions. In the Sexpertise computer programs[11] the expert knowledge is systematized from a Dutch National Institute for treatment of sexual problems.

Reviewed theories on sexuality and therapy experience with today's sexual intimacy problems are made available to everybody (Sommeling, 1990).

The computer program *Personal Sexpertise* can be used by clients (the use should be supervised by the therapist). The computer program also can be used in some way by people who do not have severe problems. In interactive games Personal Sexpertise helps the user to acquire more insight into his or her own sexual as well as communicative functioning. There are games and mini-lectures on arousal, explorations on "rules," and questions on sexual motivation. It is also possible to obtain feedback on stereotyped sex-specific roles, in the behavior "macho- or femi-score." The program supports openness on intimate topics (e.g., Figure 1 and Figure 2). A quiz analyzes the user's prejudices, exclusively medical thinking, belief in myths, etc. These games don't have the pretention to be validated tests, but will discuss attitudes and give feedback on cognition and traditional myths about sexuality (like, e.g., the famous male myths of Zilbergeld (1978). Information screens on modern contraceptives, sex problems and literature are available as well as simple exercises for treatment of anorgasmia, vaginismus, erectile failure, premature ejaculation and a tight foreskin.

Especially for professionals there is a second program: *Sexpertise Professional.* This computer program offers support to therapists, social workers and general practitioners in the field of intake assessment and treatment of sexual problems. Also more "recent" problems, like incest, sexual abuse, AIDS and problems related to female emancipation are talked about here. Of course, a therapist can never be replaced by a computer.

Without reducing the therapeutic encounter however, the program may prevent the therapist from overlooking some essential questions. Some reflections about options for treatment are added (individual, partner, sex- or communication-therapy). Reported effects of medication on sexual dysfunctions are pointed out.

Installed on data-bank or TV-teletext, the information in these computer programs is easily accessible, twenty-four hours a day (Figure 3). Already available comparative examples in the field of sexology are the Human Sexuality Computer Service in New York

FIGURE 3. Computerized information on-line (databank) or on diskette. Screen of Sexpertise, installed in a waiting room.

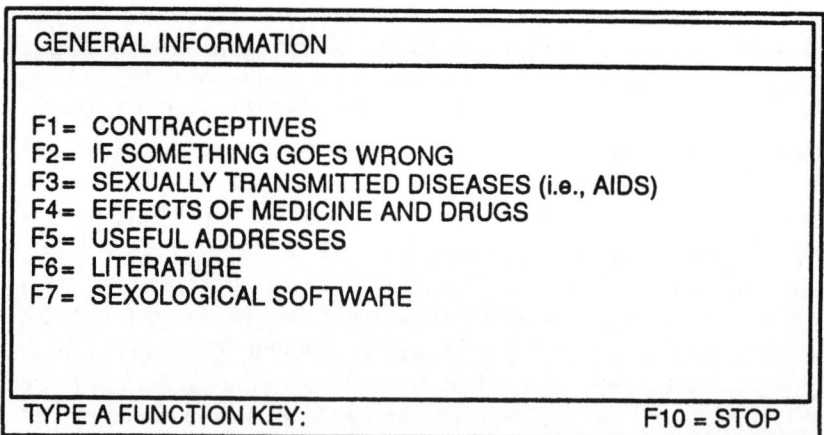

```
┌────────────────────────────────────────────────────────────┐
│ GENERAL INFORMATION                                          │
│                                                              │
│  F1 = CONTRACEPTIVES                                         │
│  F2 = IF SOMETHING GOES WRONG                                │
│  F3 = SEXUALLY TRANSMITTED DISEASES (i.e., AIDS)             │
│  F4 = EFFECTS OF MEDICINE AND DRUGS                          │
│  F5 = USEFUL ADDRESSES                                       │
│  F6 = LITERATURE                                             │
│  F7 = SEXOLOGICAL SOFTWARE                                   │
│                                                              │
│                                                              │
├────────────────────────────────────────────────────────────┤
│ TYPE A FUNCTION KEY:                            F10 = STOP   │
└────────────────────────────────────────────────────────────┘
```

with one and a half million members of their electronic meetings (Lewis, 1986); the Minitel program Sexolog in Paris with a thousand consultations per month (Waynberg, 1989); and the here mentioned Sexpertise programs in Rotterdam, Holland. Professionals or laymen can get information or put, during day or night, questions in an electronic mail box and be answered in a matter of days.

The Sexpertise program as outlined here reports in the period 09-89 till 12-90, a monthly average of 345 consultations. In an inquiry 70% of general practitioners are intended to consult the programs 4-20 times a year. The professional version is used by therapists, in some clinics and also for training programs. The personal version–next to use at home and in the context of therapy–has now been used for some years in introductory weeks for entering university students.

This article outlines some perspectives for treatment of today's sexual problems of couples. A paradigm is suggested and concrete applications are described. I hope that both, this article and the computer programs will be a contribution to the solution of a typical problem of our time: finding a way for self confident women and men–both modern autonomous beings–to lead a life of inner freedom and intimacy together.

NOTES

1. A favorable exception is the journal *Psychotherapy*, Volume 27/Fall 1990/Number 3.

2. Pesso: "Lacking adequate experience of limit-imposing interactions, the child is unsure of his or her own boundaries and vulnerable to a sense of omnipotence on the one hand and powerlessness on the other."

3. In a lecture at the World Congress of Sexology, Amsterdam, 1991.

4. For homosexual couples these problems are more or less comparable. When in heterosexual couples it is the female partner who has more outspoken sexual needs, paradoxically it is my experience that there is probably a problem of a different nature, which lies beyond the scope of this article.

5. A Jesuit adage (St. Ignace of Loyola).

6. We tend to think, stereotypically of men as coming to rapid arousal and being "mechanical" in sexual activity; it is also possible for women to behave in a similar manner.

7. The solophase can be perceived as a metaphor for the existential aloneness of people. The concepts of solophase and individuation are related associatively.

Only when individuation is developed to autonomy are people able to communicate truly and intimately.

8. Primary problems always were there, secondary problems arise later on after periods of no problem.

9. Autonomy is a discussed concept. We don't have in view the 19th century concept of a liberal moral culture. Within a Kantian tradition it is through dominating our emotional lives that we assert our autonomy, which is a feature of reason alone. True autonomy has to transcendent false polarities, it is both dependent and independent, emotional and rational, tender as well as strong (Seidler, 1988). It is adult "stand on your own." Autonomy and individuation are different things: autonomy is the area of the real self, individuation is the boundary of that area.

10. According to Whitaker and Lieberman (1964) each group session is a compromise between a wish and an anxiety. By describing these successive Group Focal Conflicts we "discovered" the stages.

11. You can order an English copy of Personal Sexpertise by paying $ 65.–to Amro Bank–Groningen, the Netherlands, number 46.72.63.787, mentioning the disk format (5.25 or 3.5). The programs are IBM-compatible. If you are interested in translation of Sexpertise Professional, write to the Publisher: Mediware, software for healthcare, Zernikepark 2, 9747 AN Groningen, the Netherlands, tel. 50-745707, fax (31)50-634556. Author's address: Louis Sommeling, Eikenlaan 45, 9321 GC Peize, the Netherlands (Fax: University, Sommeling, 50-637111).

INFORMATION

Publisher of the Sexpertise computer programs: Mediware, Groningen, the Netherlands. More information: see note 11.

AUTHOR NOTE

Louis Sommeling is author of Volumes in the Computer Assisted Humanistic Psychology Applications Series (Sexpertise and Dreamanalysis). At present he is working on a book about Male Desire.

REFERENCES

Aghassy, G. (1984). *Sexual contact between client and psychotherapist.* University, Amsterdam.

Aghassy, G. and Noot, M. (1990). *Sexuele kontakten binnen psychologische hulpverleningsrelaties.* Ministerie van Sociale Zaken en Werkgelegenheid. Den Haag.

Binik, Y. (1988). Intelligent computer-base assessment and psychotherapy. An expert system for sexual dysfunction. *Journal of Nervous and Mental Disease, 176,* 387-400. Williams and Wilkins. Baltimore: Preston.

Everaerd, W. and Dekker, J. (1981). A comparison of sex therapy and communication therapy: Couples complaining of orgastic dysfunction. In: *Journal of Sex and Marital Therapy*, 7, 278-289.

Fisher, S. (1973). *Female orgasm. Psychology, physiology and fantasy.* New York: Basic Books. (Summary in the Penguinbook: *Understanding the female orgasm.*)

Kaplan, H. (1974). *The new sex therapy.* New York: Brunner/Mazel.

Lewis, H. and M. (1986). *The electronic confessional: a sex book of the 80's.* New York: Clinical Communications, Inc. By arrangement with M. Evans and Company, Inc.

Masters W. and Johnson, V. (1966). *Human sexual response.* Boston: Little, Brown.

Nelson, J. (1991). *Male sexuality and masculine spirituality.* Subcongress Sex and Religion of the World Congress of Sexology, Amsterdam. (The subcongressproceedings will be published 1992. Amsterdam-Atlanta: Ridopi).

Ibid. (1988). *Male sexuality, masculine spirituality.* Philadelphia: The Westminster Press.

Pesso, A. and Crandell, J. (1992). *Moving psychotherapy.* Brookline Books.

Reitman, R. (1984). The use of small computers in self help sex therapy. In M. Schwartz: *Using computers in clinical practice.* New York: The Haworth Press, Inc.

Schwartz, M. (1984). *Using computers in clinical practice.* New York: The Haworth Press, Inc.

Schmidt, G. (1974). Sexuele motivation und kontrolle. *Sexual Medizin*, 3, 60-65.

Seidler, V. (1988). Fathering, authority and masculinity. In: Chapman, R. and Rutherford, J., *Male order, unwrapping masculinity.* London: Lawrence and Wishart.

Sommeling, L. (1990). Treatment of sexual problems in group dynamic groups for couples. *Dutch Journal of Group Psychotherapy*, 25, 3, 3-10.

Sommeling, L. (1990). Computer assisted treatment of sexual problems. *Journal of Dutch Sexology*, 14, 29-38.

Sommeling, L. (1991). Shaping male sexual desire. *Journal of Dutch Sexology*, 16, 174-183.

Tripp, C. (1976). *The homosexual matrix.* New York: New American Library.

Vennix, P. (1981). De regels van het spel. In N. Amsberg, Zin en onzin over seks. Deventer, Holland: v. Loghum Slaterus.

Whitaker, D. and Lieberman, M. (1964). *Psychotherapy through the group process.* Chicago: Aldine Publishing Company.

Waynberg, J. (1989). Sexolog–a computerized information service on sexuality. In: *Entre nous*, 13, 11-14.

Winnicot, D. (1965). *The maturational processes and the facilitating environment.* London: Hogarth Press.

Zilbergeld, B. (1978). *Male sexuality.* Boston: Little, Brown.

The Mating Game:
What We Know
and What We Don't Know

Joan Atwood

SUMMARY. Mate selection processes of couples have been of interest to a multitude of disciplines ranging from biology to psychology to social psychology. Debates usually center around "like marries like" or "opposites attract." While generally the research indicates, at least with regard to social variables, that similarities among couples is the norm, little systematic empirical research exists which examined this basic belief. Family therapists, also adhering to this basic assumption in their notions of couple selection, collusion, and reciprocal patterns of interaction, have not empirically tested this assumption either. The present paper examines the literature from the biological, psychological, and social psychological disciplines and discusses these assumptions in family therapy theory. A discussion of the implications for couple therapy is then presented.

Who mates with whom has been a subject of intense interest among researchers ranging from biology to psychology to social

Joan Atwood, PhD, CSW, is Coordinator of the Graduate Programs in Marriage and Family Therapy and Director of the Marital and Family Clinic at Hofstra University, Hempstead, NY 11550. She is the author of *Treatment Techniques for Common Mental Disorders* (NY: Aronson, 1987) and *Family Therapy: A Cognitive-Behavioral Approach* (release 2/92), has done extensive research and written numerous journal articles in the field of marriage and family therapy.

[Haworth co-indexing entry note]: "The Mating Game: What We Know and What We Don't Know," Atwood, Joan. Co-published simultaneously in the *Journal of Couples Therapy* (The Haworth Press, Inc.) Vol. 4, No. 1/2, 1993, pp. 61-87; and: *Attraction and Attachment: Understanding Styles of Relationships* (ed: Barbara Jo Brothers) The Haworth Press, Inc., 1993, pp. 61-87. Multiple copies of this article/chapter may be purchased from The Haworth Document Delivery Center [1-800-3-HAWORTH; 9:00 a.m. - 5:00 p.m. (EST)].

61

psychology and sociology. Although researchers have proposed numerous theories to describe the processes by which individuals select their mates, these processes have received little systematic scientific scrutiny. After reviewing the literature, these theorists from the different disciplines primarily adhere to a position analogous to "like marries like." While the biological, psychological, and social psychological theorists agree that this is generally the case, family therapists, who also have never systematically empirically tested this belief hold strongly to a similar position in their notion of equal levels of psychological maturity in relationships. It is the purpose of this paper to briefly review the current findings of the mate selection literature and examine this assumption in family therapy theory and discuss its implications for couple therapy.

BIOLOGICAL THEORIES OF MATE SELECTION

Biological theories of *evolution and natural selection* influenced theories of marital choice. Darwin's theory of sexual selection suggested that individuals competed with members of their own sex for reproductively relevant resources held by members of the opposite sex (Buss, 1988); Campbell (1886) believed that scientific matchmaking was unnecessary because evolution weeded out mismatchings of the race; and Weininger argued that a man possesses predominantly masculine characteristics in his cells and some female cells and that each characteristic seeks its opposite in the opposite sex; hence a purely masculine type would be drawn to a purely feminine type. Other biologists such as Westermarck (1936) stated that monogamy was the most advanced evolutionary form of marriage; other forms such as polygamy were survivors of earlier stages of evolutionary development; while Szondi (1937) proposed the theory that marital choice is directed by the *latent recessive genes*, by the common ancestors that reappear and formally reincarnate in later generations after having been repressed for periods.

Biological explanations of mate selection also tend to center around *instinct* or *genetics*. Here, biologists believe that instincts are basic to human behavior and are at the basis for male/female mate selection. Related to the theory of instinct is the genetic similarity theory (Rushton, Russell, and Wells, 1985) which states that genetically similar others have a tendency to seek each other out and provide supportive environments. Biologist Weinrich (1957) takes instinct theory a step further and puts forth a sociobiological "courtship theory" where he discusses courtship as the series of steps and signals by which two individuals communicate and perhaps consummate their desires to have sexual relations.

Another biologist, Trivers (1972), posits that mate selection is driven in part by different levels of investment by males and females in their offspring (Bateman, 1948). He believes that in species with much parental involvement, such as *Homo Sapiens* (Alexander and Norman, 1979), the females seek to mate with males who have the ability and willingness to provide resources related to parental investment such as food, shelter, territory, and protection. Males prefer attributes in potential females associated with reproductive value or fertility (Buss, 1987). Biologist Dyer (1988) has examined the notion of "love at first sight," i.e., physical attraction or *"sexual chemistry."* He pointed out that when individuals are sexually aroused, or when they meet someone who they define as attractive, their sympathetic nervous systems begin to create two hormones–norepinephrine and dopamine. These hormones affect the pleasure center in the brain and are directly responsible for what people feel when they report that they have "fallen in love."

SOCIAL PSYCHOLOGICAL THEORIES
OF MATE SELECTION

At a more macro level of analysis, sociologists also believe that mate selection is determined; but, instead of instincts or genetic similarity being the causal factor, they posit that sociocultural factors act as filters which help to define a pool of eligible spouse candidates from which a choice is then made (Eckland, 1982). The bulk of the sociological literature on mate selection centers around the dispute between those who claim that "opposites attract" and that "like attracts like." Sociologists have found that correlations exist between several physical and social characteristics and mate selection. These characteristics are: age, social class, residential propinquity, socioeconomic status, ethnicity, intelligence, race, religion, education, physical attractiveness, personality variables, self-concept, self-esteem, similar role definitions, similar values and social exchange. Generally, these theorists believe that the tendency to marry someone like oneself, at least in terms of macro social criteria, is very strong (Buss, 1985).

Age is highly correlated between mates. In the United States, most single persons select their mates from a closely related age group. In 1989, the median age at first marriage was 24.4 for males and 22.5 for females (U.S. Bureau of the Census, 1989). With regard to *social class*, there is a definite and marked tendency for individuals to marry within their own socioeconomic group (Eckland, 1982). Sociologists have also found that many individuals select their marriage partners from among those who live near them *geographically* (residential propinquity). People marry people who are socially and economically similar. In 1960, about three quarters of the married couples in the United States were of the same *ethnicity*. However, Carter and Glick (1976) state that with the continuous advances in communication, mobility, and the resultant increased assimilation, ethnic homogamy could conceivably approach chance levels by the fourth generation. Assortive mating for *intelligence* yields mixed results. For a review of studies done in this area, please see Richardson, 1939; Snyder, 1966; Vandenberg, 1972; and Watkins and Meredith, 1981.

Nowhere are homogamy norms more widely held to than in the area of *race*. Even though the number of interracial husbands has been on the rise since 1960 for most combinations of races, they still only involve one percent of all marriages with most interracially married couples being Black-White couples, involving primarily black husbands and white wives (Leslie & Korman, 1989; Murstein, 1986; and White and Hatcher, 1986). Studies have found that the number of people who marry within their own *religion* is far greater than chance occurrence can explain. However, this could be changing. While rates of religious intermarriage rates began to increase during the 1960's and 1970's, they skyrocketed during the 1980's. In 1985, it was estimated that 27.6 percent of all marriages were interfaith marriages. Half of all Catholics, half of all Protestants, and one third of all Jews now marry outside their respective faiths (Davis-Brown et al., 1987). With regard to *education*, there appears to be a greater likelihood for men and women with similar levels of education to pair (Bentler and Newcomb, 1978; and Murstein, 1986). When they do differ, males tend to marry females of slightly lower educational achievement (Jacobsohn and Methany, 1962).

Physical attractiveness appears to play an important role in mate selection within a community of eligible mates with similar sociocultural characteristics. Buss and Barnes (1986), in their study of mate preferences, found that physical attractiveness was ranked fourth out of thirteen available characteristics that subjects had to choose from to describe an ideal mate. The physically attractive characteristic was preferred significantly more by men than by women (Buss and Barnes, 1986). Most of the studies in this area indicate that as courtship continues, couples differing in attractiveness are more likely to break up than those more similar in attractiveness (Feingold, 1981; Folkes, 1982; Murstein and Christy, 1976; Price and Vandenberg, 1980; and White, 1980). Kalick and Hamilton (1986) found that while people may prefer highly attractive partners, "real world considerations" (p. 675) result in the necessity of most people to lower their expectations and to couple with others having a level of attractiveness similar to their own.

Kendrick, Sadalla, Groth, and Trost (1990) found that females were more selective overall particularly on status linked variables. Males had lower requirements for a sexual partner than did females but were nearly selective as females when considering a long-term partner. Similarly, Townsend and Levy (1990) found that women are more likely to prefer or insist that sexual intercourse occur in relationships that involve affection and marital potential, and women place more potential than men do on partner's masculine traits such as employment, financial, and intellectual status, and valued commitment in a relationship more highly than men did (Davis, 1990). Men emphasized stereotypically desirable feminine traits (appearance). These findings were supported by Buss (1989).

A careful review of the studies examining *personality variables* indicates that personality traits are moderately matched for couples but that no one variable stands out as being consistently related to high assortive matching. (For a review of these studies, please see Centers, 1975; Farley and Mueller, 1978; Price and Vandenberg, 1980; and Sindberg and Roberts, 1972.) The role of *self-concept* in the mate selection process is an important factor. Mittlemen (1956) proposed that individuals enter relationships which reaffirm their self-concepts. Thus, the manner in which individuals perceive their own capabilities and limitations may influence their behavior within their social environment in terms of initiating a relationship with a potential mate.

Social psychologists also present theories of mate selection. For example, they believe that *role and value agreement* are other factors involved in mate selection. According to role theory, persons would tend to choose mates on the basis of courtship and marital role agreement. The role itself is not as important as the consensus of the partners with regard to the role (Eshleman, 1988). Similarly, value theory posits that interpersonal attraction is facilitated when the partners share or perceive themselves as sharing similar values (Berscheid and Hatfield, 1978). Other social psychologists believe that positive and negative social exchanges are related to whether or not a dating relationship will endure. *Social exchange theory* states that enduring love and attraction are most likely to develop when each person in a relationship perceives an advantageous exchange between received and contributed resources (Thibaut and Kelly, 1959). A variation of this theory was put forth by Centers (1975) who stated that in any relationship individuals attempt to pair with someone with whom association brings the most rewards and the fewest costs. Kerckhoff and Davis (1962) hypothesized that certain social attributes and personality relationships operate differently depending on the particular stage of courtship. The results of their study indicate that value consensus operates in the early stages of courtship and need-complementarity later on. However, further replication (Levinger, Senn, and Jorgensen, 1970) has failed to support this theory.

One of the first social psychologists to focus on the on-going development of relationships was Ira Reiss (1960) who postulated a *wheel theory of love.* He stated that the spokes of the wheel are rapport, self revelation, mutual dependency and personality need fulfillment. These are the necessary stages leading to persons falling in love. The wheel spirals and this leads to increasingly deeper rapport, and greater self revelation, and so forth. It may also unwind leading to less rapport, which successively weakens each stage. Theorists have found that a norm of reciprocity develops so that the levels of intimacy revealed are comparable (Worthy, Gary, and Kahn, 1969) and are also related to the extent of love (Rubin, Kill, Peplau and Durkel-Schette, 1980) lending support to the theory.

Another sequential type theory was developed by Murstein (1970). Murstein's basic premise is that mate selection results from a bargaining process in which self-acceptance is considered a negotiable asset. Murstein suggested that most couples pass through three stages before they marry. People are at first attracted to each other by their perceptions of their attractive qualities. This is referred to as the *"stimulus"* stage and is highly influenced by physical attractiveness. Next, they enter into the *"value"* stage where they begin to discover whether they share similar values and attitudes. If there is agreement, the relationship progresses to the *"role"* stage. At this point, the couple's interaction provides them with a good idea of what they would be like if they were married. Solomon (1986) recently examined and found support for some of Murstein's original hypotheses. Cate and Koval (1983) questioned the adequacy of all the sequential models and pointed out that replications have not provided much support for the hypothesized stages. In addition, they suggested that in many cases dating proceeded into a marital relationship without much intimacy, and that often external factors such as social pressures and lack of attractive alternatives propel relationships to marriage.

In sum, as Buss (1985) believes: assortive mating is the most common human deviation from random mating in Western societies. In general age, education, race, religion, and ethnic background show the strongest assortment. The findings in this area are:

1. Males and females generally marry those who are similar in age. When there is a discrepancy, males are usually slightly older.
2. Males and females generally marry those with similar education. As with age, when there is a discrepancy, males usually are more educated.
3. Males and females usually marry those of a similar race although this is changing with slightly more interracial marriages occurring.
4. Males and females generally marry those of a similar religion although this is changing with more interreligious marriages occurring.

5. Males and females usually marry those with a similar ethnic background, although there have been major differences occurring within the past thirty years with individuals from dissimilar ethnic backgrounds marrying.

These stronger sociological similarities are followed by the social psychological variables of intelligence, personality variables, self-concept, self-esteem, values, and physical attractiveness.

PSYCHOLOGICAL THEORIES OF MATE SELECTION

Psychodynamic Theories of Mate Selection

The psychoanalytic perspective views the composition and quality of courtship, mate selection, and marriage as being dependent on the quality of personality development that each partner has achieved (Eisenstein, 1956). Those individuals who have developed a differentiated and individuated sense of self are predicted to experience a positive marital relationship. Well adjusted individuals are believed to achieve this quality of personality organization by successfully managing a series of developmental processes. Consequently, prediction of marital choice is reportedly possible by understanding one's early personality development and interpersonal experiences (Poalino and McCrady, 1978).

Freud (1914) believed that a person tended to fall in love with and marry a person similar to their opposite sexed parent. This is generally unconscious and centers around the Oedipal/Electra Complex. For Freud (1921), the concept of falling in love involved the operation of intense narcissistic needs. The intermeshing and responsiveness of these needs is a significant factor in the choice of a mate. An individual is apt to seek out, consciously and unconsciously, another individual who promises to provide gratification for the unconscious narcissistic needs (Meissner, 1978). Benedek (1959) concluded that lovers offer each other an exchange of ego ideals. Ohmann (1947) stated that people fall in love with individuals who provide the missing parts of the personality which are felt as ego deficiencies. Reik (1957) posited that, "One falls in love when one is dissatisfied with oneself and meets someone of the opposite sex who has those characteristics that he or she desires but has been unable to achieve" (p. 321). Through identification with such an individual, one's perceived deficiencies (the individuals' failures to attain their own ego ideal) are eliminated.

Hartmann (1950) delineated three levels of object relations: primary narcissism, need gratification, and object constancy. Persons at the first two levels have numerous difficulties in a marital situation. Blanck and Blanck (1968) considered the struggle to differentiate oneself a continuous struggle throughout life. They believe that mature love is only possible when the individual had a firm sense of identity. Mahler, Pine, and Bergman (1975) provided analytic theorists with the separation-individuation process whereby the child separated him/herself from the symbiotic relationship with the mother and learned to tolerate both aloneness and non-symbiotic closeness. Other theorists have utilized the separation-individuation process in their discussions of mate selection (see Blanck and Blanck, 1968; Gans, 1975; Joffe and Sandler, 1965; Roth-Puckett, 1977; and Winestone, 1973).

Thus, those individuals who are psychologically ready for marriage are considered to be at the object constancy level of object relations (Hartmann, 1950), having passed successfully through the psychosexual stages of development (Freud, 1914), and to some degree, to have successfully mastered the separation-individuation process (Mahler, 1965). Those individuals who have not mastered the developmental tasks preceding marriage are said to attempt to complete themselves through a spouse (Freud, 1925); exchange ego ideals (Benedek, 1959; Jung, 1953; and Reik, 1957), attempt to protect themselves from hunger and aloneness (Schor and Sanville, 1978), and to distort their perceptions of their spouse in order to fill in the gaps of their personality (Satir, 1967).

While the above theorists presented discussions concerning the development of the capacity to successfully love another person, the following theorist discusses what attracts individuals to each other. While most theorists postulate that mate selection is due to homogeneity in attitudes and personality traits (Burgess and Wallin, 1953), Winch proported that it is due to complementary needs. Winch (1952, 1955, 1958) and Winch, Ktones, and Ktones, (1954) postulated the *theory of complementarity of needs*. These authors incorporated sociological findings with regard to background factors and psychoanalytic concepts concerning personality development. This theory states that potential mates are first selected out of a "field of eligibles" which is originally developed through homogamy of social factors. Their belief was that even though mate selection is homogamous with respect to age, social class, residential propinquity, race, religion, education, physical attractiveness, etc., when it comes to psychological needs, mate selection tends to be complementary rather than homogamous. Later research in this area of assortive mate selection has concentrated on correspondence between partners (e.g., Johnson, Ahern, and Cole, 1980; and Watkins and Meredith, 1981) especially as it influences personal environment (Synder and Gangestad, 1982) and adult personality development (Buss, 1984). Thus, Winch believes that beyond the initial similarities, mates are selected by means of "heterogamy of motives." Heterogamy of motives refers to the concept of need complementarity (Gurman, 1978). However, the vast majority of research has generally failed to support Winch (see Murstein, 1976).

Family Theorists

Other clinicians have adopted a different theory of need complementarity with regard to the mate selection process (Aldous, 1973; Aroaz, 1974; Dicks, 1967; Napier, 1971, 1988; and Sager, 1976). While Winch's theory focuses on *individual* selection factors (why A chose B), the above listed clinicians have attempted to address the process of how and why A and B choose each other as a *joint* decision. Unlike the intrapersonal psychoanalytic position stated earlier, these theorists examine the interpersonal process of mate selection. This unspoken process is referred to as "collusion" (Dicks, 1967; Willi, 1982); "family projection process" (Bowen, 1966); "pseudo-identification" (Eidelberg, 1948); "trading of disassociations" (Wynne, 1971); or merging (Boszormenyi-Nagy and Framo, 1967). These theorists suggest that an unconscious collaboration exists where each partner chooses the other and enters into an implicit agreement to fulfill the other's needs (Sager, 1976).

Similarly, Miller, Nunnally and Wackman (1988) offers a theory of mate selection that is founded on the notion that individuals choose partners who have similar concepts of the meaning of a relationship. Driven by a desire to form an interpersonal union, individuals choose each other as partners in such a way that their own habits, feelings and ideals are confirmed. The formation of this union is structured by the concept of collusion which encompasses the notions that partners are joined on the basis of similar kinds of unresolved conflicts around which an unadmitted and hidden interplay occurs. It is in this interplay that the partners take on roles which create an impression that they are, characteristically, opposites of each other. But, in actuality, they are "polarized variants of the same conflict" (p. 107).

Perhaps the most detailed process of mate selection is presented by the object relations family theorists (Dicks, 1967; Fairbairn, 1952; Willi, 1982, 1984; Slipp, 1984, 1988; and Scharf and Scharf, 1957). Psychoanalytically oriented marital therapy theory focuses on the unconscious determinants of marital choice (Nadelson, 1978). "The process of selecting a mate is not magical or mystical but an expression of each individual's personal needs and development in a particular sociocultural context" (Nicols and Everett, 1986). The object relations theorists, like the earlier psychoanalytic theorists, address the concept of the unconscious as being an active agent in mate selection. Dicks (1967), Fairbairn (1952, 1963), and Ackerman (1958) discuss in detail how individuals choose partners based on their own previous relationships with significant objects in their early lives. Willi (1984) states, "Collusive partner choice does not appear to be a key-in-lock process where both personalities fit tightly together. Instead, the couple emerges as a result of mutual adjustment, a blending of the latent and manifest personality traits of both partners" (p. 161). Ackerman (1958) stated, "Particularly significant is the disguised motivational element of searching out a mate who is likely to assuage or counteract one's personal anxiety . . . it is often said that one neurotic marries another . . . it is common knowledge that the neurotic tendency of one marital partner often complements that of the other . . . When one partner exhibits pathological anxiety responses, the other usually does too" (p. 165).

Dicks (1967) saw the obscure process of mate selection as being based on unconscious signals or cues by which partners recognize the other's "fitness" for joint working through or repeating of still unresolved splits or conflicts inside each other's persons–at the same time paradoxically sensing the guarantee that with that person, they (conflicts) will not be worked through. Family therapist Boszormenyi-Nagy (1965) commented, "What appears to be true feedback between two partners may actually be programmed by their internal relational events. Many marriages are essentially lived between each partner and their respective introjects" (p. 110). Framo (1982) agrees, "Each partner unconsciously attempts to maneuver the other into some earlier relationship pattern in their family of origin: each has a disquieting feeling that some old tormenting ghost has risen to haunt him. Of course, the partner must cooperate to complete the process needed to maintain the relationship" (p. 89).

Minuchin (1974) does not necessarily describe a particular theory of mate selection; however, he speaks of a process of mutual accommodation or patterned transactions. It is through these patterned transactions that each spouse triggers and monitors the behaviors of the other and is in turn influenced by the previous behavioral sequence. These transactional patterns form an invisible web of complementary demands that regulate family situations "When partners join, each expects the actions of the spouse to take the forms with which he is familiar. Each spouse will try to organize the other spouse along lines that are familiar or preferred, and will push the other to accommodate" (p. 27).

Virginia Satir (1988) discussed some of the effects of previous relationships on an individual's choice of a partner. "Without necessarily knowing it, parents are the architects of their children's romantic and sexual selves. I believe that two people are first interested in each other because of their sense of sameness, but they remain interested over the years because of their ability to enjoy differences" (Satir, 1988, p. 154). Another experiential family therapist, Carl Whitaker, states, "If you assume that the beginning of the marriage is a transference phenomenon, then the choice of a marital partner is infinitely accurate: It's unconscious to the unconscious" (Neill and Kniskern, 1982, p. 173). According to Whitaker, mate selection is done with the same kind of exactness that you would expect of a computer. The combination of a husband and a wife is an extremely accurate one.

Kirschner and Kirschner (1986) have given some consideration to the way individuals seek out and choose a mate. Their theory is based on the notion that spouses extend their self-definition to include the other. Part of the self and/or parts of the personalities of the parental figures are projected onto or unconsciously assigned to a mate. Spouses choose partners similar to parental figures who are also able to provide the reparental inputs they need. The Kirschners also place significance on the role of the family of origin in determining a mate. They believe that "Marriage involves a thrust toward completion and integration of the self. Spouses are chosen not only on the basis of congruency in self-system structures, but also out of a longing to promote growth of self and the other" (p. 148). Scarf (1987) states that although the choice of the marital partner often seems to have been made very quickly, on the basis of little conscious knowledge, it turns out with great accuracy of complementarity and facts of personalities and even life experiences of the partners. Couples quite often turn out to have striking similarities in terms of childhood experiences. She believes that the marriage partner is a person who connects us to parts of our beings which are completely suppressed, lost to memory, and yet well remembered at an almost cellular level. Nicols and Everett (1980) describe the mate selection process as one in which an individual's level of personal development and historical need patterns link with those of a mate in a new dyadic process.

Napier (1988) who gives considerable emphasis to the process of mate selection states, "If there is any single principle in our selection of mates, it is in my view that we marry someone who is a kind of psychological twin. We are all indeed in search of someone who will help us feel psychologically complete" (Napier, 1988, p. 218). "We are attracted to someone whose basic psychological situation in his/her family of origin is similar to our own. That is, we identify with this person's core problems, dynamics that were shaped in the early family" (Napier, 1988, p. 221).

Hendrix (1988) believes that in psychological development from infant to adult a part of ourselves is repressed. He calls this the "lost self," the part that is repressed due to its unacceptability. As individuals reach maturity they seek to fill an emptiness inside themselves caused by this repressed side of the personality. As a result, individuals seek mates whose personalities are complementary to their own. They have a template, "Imago," of what they long for in a partner which in reality is the composite of all their impressions of their original caretakers. When individuals find someone who matches this imago, they become intensely excited because their unconscious believes that this relationship will provide the nurturing they have been longing for and in this manner they will regain their original wholeness.

Behavioral family therapists Jacobson and Margolin (1979) also believe that often a relationship is based on one's fantasy that a spouse will provide the complementary behavior lacking in oneself. Stuart (1980) addressed the theory of assortive mate selection in noting that "like marries like" (p. 77). Buss (1985) believes that ". . . it is rare to find partners who are more than two developmental levels art. That amount of developmental discrepancy usually leads to separation and divorce" (p. 16). In fact, Mehrabian (1989) after an extensive review of the literature, found that there was greater interspouse similarity in stable compared with unstable marriages.

Papp (1983) discusses the relationship between spouses in terms of their patterns of reciprocity. She quotes several other researchers and clinicians who address reciprocity in relationships. Reciprocity is viewed as interlocking collusion (Winch, Ktones, and Ktones, 1954), "reciprocal functioning" (Bowen, 1960); "pseudo-mutuality" (Wynne et al., 1958); "complementarity" (Jackson, 1957); "bilateral reciprocity" (Dicks, 1967), "need complementarity" (Mittleman, 1944), "hidden agenda" (Sager, 1967), "pattern of reciprocal overadequacy and inadequacy" (Bowen, 1978), and "unconscious deal" (Framo, 1982). Haley (1963) describes the reciprocity in a relationship as one partner taking the helpless dependent position in order to control the other partner and balance the hierarchical power structure.

Jackson's (1957) original notion of "complementarity" was further explicated by Watzlawick, Beavin, and Jackson (1967). These latter authors note their work was preceded by Bateson's (1958) description of relationship interactions in New Guinea tribes. The similarity of complementarity and Bowen's reciprocal functioning may be seen in Watzlawick et al.'s "dominant" and "adaptive" spouse stances. Watzlawick et al. (1967) relate that in a complementary pair, there is an "inequality" in the relationship often based on one partner being "one up" and the other "one down." They also use the term "symmetrical interaction" to describe relationships said to be "equal" (i.e., the members of the pair are similar in their behavior and there is "minimization of difference" (p. 68-69). Watzlawick et al. (1967) also use the term "metacomplementary" to describe relationships in which "A" lets or forces "B" to be in charge of him (p. 69). This statement seems quite similar to Bowen's (1976) suggestion that in a marital pair, "one may assume the adaptive role and force the other to be dominant" (p. 79).

The outcome of these relationship patterns also appears to have similarity if one considers Watzlawick, Beavin and Jackson's (1967) and Bowen's (1960, 1976, 1978) writings. The former authors see symmetry as leading to conflict if members of the pair try to be "more equal" or one up each other in a "symmetrical escalation" (Watzlawick et al., 1967, p. 107).

Bowen and Differentiation of Self

Of all the family theorists, Bowen was the most articulate about mate selection processes. A cornerstone of Bowen's theory is the concept of differentiation of self. "It defines all people, from the lowest to the highest possible level of human functioning, according to one single denominator" (1972, p. 472). Bowen's concept of differentiation refers to an individual's capacity to distinguish the feeling and the thinking processes. At the highest level are those with a separate self who can differentiate between their emotional system and intellectual system; at the lower levels are those whose intellectual and emotional systems are so fused that their lives are controlled by their emotional system. Bowen states that these individuals are flooded with feelings which prevent them from separating thoughts from feelings. They always look for togetherness in relationships and become amorphous "no selfs" in regard to their own beliefs and convictions. It is interesting to note that what is valued in Bowen's system are the qualities for which men are socialized and what is devalued are those for which women are socialized.

Bowen (1961, 1966, 1976, 1978) believed that clinical experience suggests that individuals tend to choose marital partners who have achieved an equivalent level of maturity, but who have adopted opposite patterns of defensive organization (Meissner, 1978). Bowen believed that mating, marriage, and reproduction are governed to a significant degree by emotional and instinctual forces. The way in which an individual handles these forces in dating and courtship and in timing and planning of marriage provide one of the best views of differentiation of the spouses (Bowen, 1978).

These levels of differentiation are determined by the time s/he leaves the family of origin (Gurman, 1978). An individual's level of differentiation is a crucial factor in determining a potential spouse. "People pick spouses who have the same level of differentiation" (Bowen, 1978, p. 376). Based on this premise, the selection of a mate is not accidental. Each individual has the tendency to repeat the style of relating learned in the parental family in all future relationships. In this regard, poorly differentiated individuals seek out equally dependent relationships in which they can borrow enough strength to function (Bowen, 1976). According to Bowen (1961, 1966, 1976, 1978), "Individuals seek a partner based on the ability of that partner to help the individual repeat early family experiences, the partner's level of differentiation, and the expectation that the partner will help the individual make up for the developmental failures" (Gurman, 1978). According to his theory, an individual's level of differentiation is fundamental to his/her selection of a mate in that individuals are predisposed to marry others with levels of differentiation similar to their own (Atwood, 1992; Goldenberg and Goldenberg, 1991).

Similar to the object relations theorists, Bowen (1961) discusses opposite patterns of defensive organization to the levels of differentiation as necessary factors in selecting a mate. He states that one spouse or partner will assume a dominant role in response to the other assuming an adaptive role or vice versa. Bowen believes that these roles are not determined by gender but in response to the position each partner maintained in his/her family of origin. These characteristics play a major role in the original choice of each other as partners (Bowen, 1978, p. 377).

Blatt and Wild (1976) emphasized the role of boundaries in a discussion of differentiation. They examined the development from a state of autism to symbiotic fusion with the need gratifying object, to separation, individuation and the beginning of mature object relationships. The developmental task of differentiation was believed to be achieved in marriage after the couple has accepted and accommodated to their individual differences in style, needs, and role expectation (Pineo, 1960).

Bowen maintained that life style, thinking, and emotional patterns at various levels of the scale differed so much that people choose their spouses and close friends at equal levels of differentiation as themselves. Moynihan and Ingraham (1971), Kear (1978), and Weinberg (1978) have presented data substantiating this claim in the case of selecting a spouse. Citrin (1982) examined the relationship between individuals' level of development and interpersonal perception. He found that individuals choose their spouses at the same level of differentiation as themselves. Barnett (1971) discussed a rigid pattern which was strongly influenced by and influenced perceptions of spouses, obsessive compulsive/hysteric relationships. In this culturally reinforced relationship, the obsessive compulsive (usually the male) was attracted to the hysteric's (usually the female) aliveness and promise of emotional nurturance. The hysteric was similarly attracted to the obsessive-compulsive's structure, dependability, and intellect. In both cases, the individuals sought in each other what they have not been fully able to develop in themselves.

DISCUSSION

In order to present the reader with a general flavor for the research findings and theorizing in the area of mate selection, the biological theories of mate selection, the social psychological variables associated with mate selection, along with a discussion of the psychological theories associated with mate selection was presented. In addition, the basic assumption of family therapy theory—persons of equal levels of differentiation and psychological maturity marry—was presented. From the above discussion it is obvious that family therapy theorists hold certain assumptions around mate selection processes. Some of these major assumptions are:

1. Spouses in a relationship tend to be at equal levels of psychological maturity (Meissner, 1978; and Sonne and Swirsky, 1981).
2. People tend to recreate their interpersonal world in relationships by recreating patterns of interaction that were estab-

lished by early caretakers and maintained in family of origin systems (Ables and Brandsma, 1977; and Willi, 1984).

3. Couples collude, cooperate with each other, to maintain the relationship (Blanck and Blanck, 1968; Dicks, 1963; and Willi, 1984).

The problem is that these assumptions have yet to be systematically and empirically tested. To briefly summarize, in general, biological, psychological, and social psychological research and theories on mate selection assume that "like marries like." Family therapy theorists, building on psychodynamic or object relations family therapy theory, have consequently assumed that "like marries like" psychologically as well. Family therapy theory then takes as its basic assumption that persons of equal psychological maturity, emotionality, and self-esteem marry. While this belief has never been empirically tested by these theorists, it continues to be a cornerstone of the therapeutic practices of clinicians grounded in the family therapy paradigm.

The implications for family practice are enormous. For example, if a clinician believes that psychological equality in relationships exists, then reciprocity in couples is assumed. If there is the belief that equivalent levels of maturity/immaturity and self differentiation exist in couples, then there is the belief that there is a tendency for marital partners to be operating at equivalent levels. This puts clinicians on guard because when they find signs of pathology/dysfunction in one marital partner, they keep an eye open for inductions of a similar level of personality organization in the other. If this basic assumption that "like marries like" is incorrect, or if it is correct under only certain instances, then clinicians could be searching for (possibly creating) non-existent pathology so that what a couple therapist may mistake for pathology may in fact be complementarity.

Research which examines specific variables affecting choice of marital partners, successful and unsuccessful factors related to these specific variables and the variables which lead to "happy" lasting marriages will surely lend information on successful coupling, will help us to delineate the "workable" issues in premarital counseling, will familiarize us with the traps and pitfalls associated with unsuccessful mating, the variables related to more successful mating, and hopefully lead us to a clearer understanding of the mating game. At this time, over 55% of married individuals will eventually divorce. This rate is even higher among second marriages. Divorce is typically considered a negative state in this society as is evidenced by the high stress during the transition and the problems often associated with the children of divorce. Research which could contribute to a more detailed understanding of the mate selection process might help couples thwart off future divorce. For example, what variables are relevant in the mate selection process in the first place? What variables are important in keeping the initial attraction alive over the course of the marriage or relationship? What variables are important determinants in a couple's decision to stay together? What variables are important in determining marital satisfaction? Are there intervening variables? If yes, what are they? These and other questions would shed some light on the coupling process and in so doing help couple therapists understand couple dynamics in a more holistic way. Once therapists have a better understanding of the effects of mate selection processes, they can begin to theorize about a couple therapy that is more grounded and supported by research.

However, as Napier (1988) suggests, ". . . the process of choosing a mate is so bewilderingly complex that no one fully understands it. No one." (p. 207). Thus, while not completely a random process, i.e., there is the existence of determinable biological and social psychological patterns and correlations, it appears that mate selection is not either a fully conscious process in that it is strongly influenced by individual psychological perception and definition. It is this aspect of the mate selection process that appears to limit our ability to fully understand one of the most basic of human activities: intimate interpersonal relationships.

REFERENCES

Ables, B. & Brandsma, J. (1977). *Therapy for couples.* San Francisco: Jossey-Bass.

Ackerman, N. (1958). *The psychodynamics of family life.* New York: Basic.

Aldous, N. (1973). Mechanisms of stalemate in conjoint marital therapy. *Canadian Psychiatric Association Journal, 18,* 191-197.

Alexander, R. & Norman, K. (1979). Concealment of ovulation, parental care and human social evolution. In N. Chagnon & E. Irons (Eds.) *Evolutionary biology and human social behavior: An anthropological perspective.* London: Duxbury.

Althus, W. (1970). Marriage and order of birth. *Proceedings of the Annual Convention of the American Psychological Association, 5,* 361-362.

Aroaz, D. (1974). Marital transference. *Journal of Family Counseling, 2,* 55-63.

Atwood, J. (1992). Comprehensive marital therapy. *Journal of Couples Therapy, 3, 41-65.*

Barnett, J. (1971). Narcissism and dependency in the obsessional-hysteric marriage. *Family Process, 10,* 75-83.

Bateman, A. (1948). Intrasexual selection in *Drosophila. Heredity, 2,* 349-368.

Bateson, G. (1958). *The naven.* New York: Random.

Benedek, T. (1959). Parenthood as a developmental phase. *Journal of the American Psychoanalytic Association, 7,* 374-389.

Bentler, P. & Newcomb, M. (1978). Longitudinal study of marital success and failure. *Journal of Clinical and Consulting Psychology, 46,* 1053-1070.

Berscheid, E., Dion, K., & Walter, G. (1971). Physical attractiveness and dating choice: A test of the matching hypothesis. *Journal of Experiential Social Psychology, 7,* 173-189.

Berscheld, E. & Hatfield (Walster), E. (1978). *Interpersonal attraction.* (Eds.) Reading, PA: Addison-Wesley.

Blanck, A. & Blanck, G. (1968). *Marriage and personal development.* New York: Columbia University Press.

Blatt, J. & Wild, C. (1976). *Schizophrenia: A developmental analysis.* New York: Academic Press.

Boszormenyi-Nagy, I. (1965). A theory of relationships: Experience and transaction. In I. Boszormenyi-Nagy & J. Framo (Eds.) *Intensive family therapy.* New York: Harper and Row.

Boszormenyi-Nagy, I. & Framo, J. (1967). Relational models and meanings. In G. Zuk & I. Boszormenyi-Nagy (Eds.) *Family therapy and disturbed families.* Palo Alto, CA: Science and Behavior Books.

Bowen, M. (1960). A family concept of schizophrenia. In D. Jackson (Ed.) *The etiology of schizophrenia.* New York: Basic.

Bowen, M. (1961). The use of family theory in clinical practice. *Comprehensive Psychiatry, 7,* 345-374.

Bowen, M. (1966). The use of family theory in clinical practice. *Comprehensive Psychiatry, 7,* 345-374.

Bowen, M. (1972). Toward the differentiation of a self in one's own family. In J. Framo (Ed). *Family interaction.* New York: Spring.

Bowen, M. (1976). Theory and practice of psychotherapy. In P. Guerin (Ed.) *Family therapy.* New York: Gardener Press.

Bowen, M. (1978). *Family therapy in clinical practice.* New York: Jason Aronson.

Burgess, T. & Wallin, P. (1983). *Engagement and marriage.* Philadelphia: Lippincott.

Burns, R. (1979). *The Self-Concept in theory, measurement development*. London: Longman.

Buss, D. (1984). Toward a psychology of person-environment correlation: The role of spouse selection. *Journal of Personality and Social Psychology, 47,* 361-377.

Buss, D. (1985). Human mate selection. *American Scientist, 73,* 47-51.

Buss, D. (1987). Sex differences in human mates selection. In C. Crawford, M. Smith & D. Krebe (Eds.). *Sociobiology and psychology: Issues, goals and findings*. Hillsdale, NJ: Erlbaum.

Buss, D. (1988). From vigilance to violence: Tactics of mate retention in American undergraduates. *Ethology and Sociobiology, 9,* 291-317.

Buss, D. (1989). Sex differences in human mate preferences. *Behavioral and Brain Sciences, 12,* 1-49.

Buss, D. & Barnes, M. (1986). Preferences in human mate selection. *Journal of Personality and Social Psychology, 47,* 361-377.

Campbell, G. (1886). Sir George Campbell on scientific marriage-matchmaking. *The Spectator, 59,* 1206-1207.

Carter, H. & Glick, P. (1976). *Marriage and Divorce: A social and economic study*. Cambridge, MA: Harvard University Press.

Cate, R. & Koval, J. (1983). Heterosexual relationship development: Is it really a sequential process? *Adolescence, 18,* 507-514.

Centers, R. (1975). *Sexual attraction and love: An instrument theory*. Springfield, IL: Thomas.

Citrin, R. (1982). The relationship between differentiation of self and interspousal perception. *Dissertation Abstracts International,* (University Microfilms, 82-27, 827).

Cohen, H. (1981). *Connections: Understanding social relationships*. Iowa: University of Iowa Press.

Critelli, J. & Baldwin, A. (1979). Birth order: Complementarity vs. homogamy as determinants of attraction in dating relationships. *Journal of Personality Assessment, 44,* 624-629.

Davis, S. (1990). Men as success objects and women as sex objects: A study of personal advertisements. *Sex Roles, 23,* 43-50.

Davis-Brown, K., Salamon, S. & Surra, C. (1987). Economic and social factors in mate selection: An ethnographic analysis of an agricultural community. *Journal of Marriage and the Family, 49,* 41-45.

Dicks, H. (1967). *Marital tensions*. New York: Basic Books.

Duck, S. & Gilmore, R. (Eds.) (1982). *Personal relationships 2: Developing personal relationships*. London: Academic Press.

Dyer, K. (1988). Changing patterns of marriage and mating within Australia. *Australian Journal of Sex, Marriage and Family, 9,* 107-119.

Eckland, B. (1982). Theories of mate selection. *Social Biology, 29,* 7-21.

Eidelberg, L. (1948). *Studies in psychoanalysis*. New York: Guilford Press.

Eidelberg, L. (1956). Neurotic choice of a mate. In V. Eisenstein (Ed.) *Neurotic interaction in marriage*. New York: Basic Books.

Eisenstein, V. (1956). *Neurotic interaction in Marriage.* New York: Basic.

Eshleman, J., Cashion, B. & Basirico, L. (1988). *Sociology: An introduction to the third edition.* Boston: Little, Brown.

Fairbairn, W. (1952). *Psychoanalytic studies of the personality.* London: Routledge and Kegan Paul.

Fairbairn W. (1963). Synopsis of an object relations theory of the personality. *International Journal of Psychoanalysis, 44,* 224-225.

Farley, F. & Mueller, C. (1978). Arousal, personality, and assortive mating in marriage. Generalizability and cross-cultural factors. *Journal of Sex and Marital Therapy, 4,* 50-53.

Feingold, A. (1981). Testing equity as an explanation for romantic couples "mismatched" on physical attractiveness. *Psychological Reports, 49,* 247-250.

Fitts, W. (1972). *Self concept of psychopathology.* Los Angeles: Western Psychological Services.

Folkes, V. (1982). Forming relationships and the matching hypothesis. *Personality and Social Psychology Bulletin, 8,* 631-636.

Framo, J. (1965). Rationale and techniques of intensive family therapy. In I. Boszormenyi-Nagy & J. Framo (Eds.) *Intensive family therapy.* New York: Harper and Row.

Framo, J. (1976). Family of origin as a therapeutic resource for adults in marital and family therapy. *Family Process, 15,* 193-210.

Framo, J. (1982). *Explorations in marital and family therapy.* New York: Springer.

Freud, S. (1914). On narcissism: An introduction. In *General psychological theory: Papers on metapsychology.* New York: Collier.

Gans, M. (1975). *Separation-individuation, deprivation and closeness in adult love relationships.* Unpublished doctoral dissertation, CSPP-SP.

Goldenberg, I. & Goldenberg, H. (1991). *Family therapy: An overview.* Pacific Grove, CA: Brooks/Cole.

Gurman, A. (1978). Contemporary marital therapies. In T. Poalino & B. McGrady (Eds.) *Marriage and marital therapy.* New York: Brunner/Mazel.

Hacker, A. (1979). Divorce a la mode. *New York Review of Books. 26,* 23-27.

Haley, J. (1963). Marriage therapy. *Archives of General Psychiatry, 8,* 313-334.

Haley, J. (1987). *Problem-solving therapy.* San Francisco: Jossey-Bass.

Haley, J. (1986). *Uncommon therapy: The psychiatric techniques of Milton H. Erickson.* New York: Norton.

Hartmann, H. (1950). *Ego psychology and the problem of adaptation.* New York: International University Press.

Hendrix, H. (1988). *Getting the love you want.* New York: Harper & Row.

Huston, T. (1974). *Foundations of interpersonal attraction.* New York: Random.

Jackson, D. (1957). The question of family homeostasis. *Psychiatric Quarterly, 31,* 79-90.

Jacobson, N. & Margolin, G. (1979). *Marital therapy: Strategies based on social learning theory and behavior exchange principles.* New York: Brunner/Mazel.

Jacobsohn, P. & Methany, A. (1962). Mate selection in open marriages. *Journal of Comparative Sociology, 23*, 98-123.

Joffe, W. & Sandler, J. (1965). Notes on pain, depression and individuation. *Psychoanalytic Study of the Child, 20*, 394-424.

Johnson, R., Ahern, F. & Cole, R. (1980). Secular change in degree of assortive mating for ability. *Behavior Genetics, 10*, 1-7.

Kalick, S. & Hamilton, T. (1988). Closer look at a matching simulation: Reply to Aron. *Journal of Personality and Social Psychology, 54*, 447-451.

Kear, J. (1978). Marital attraction and satisfaction as a function of differentiation of self and rigidity-flexibility to marital conflict. *Dissertation Abstracts International, 83-13*, 872.

Kenrick, D., Sadalla, E., Groth, G. & Trost, M. (1990). Evolution, traits, and the stages of human courtship: Qualifying the parental investment model. *Journal of Personality, 58*, 97-116.

Kerckhoff, A. & Davis, K. (1962). Value concerns and need complementarity in mate selection. *American Sociological Review, 27*, 295-323.

Kerr, M. (1981). Family systems theory and therapy. In A. Gurman & N. Kniskern (Eds.) *Handbook of family therapy*. New York: Brunner/Mazel.

Kirshner, S. & Kirshner, D. (1986). *Comprehensive family therapy*. New York: Brunner/Mazel.

Kleinke, C. (1975). *First impression: The psychology of encountering others*. Englewood Cliffs, NJ: Prentice-Hall.

Kramer, R. & Akhtar, S. (1988). The developmental context of internalized object relations and clinical applications of Mahler's theory of symbiosis and separation-individuation. *Psychoanalytic Quarterly, 57*, 547-574.

Leslie, G. & Korman, S. (1989). *The family in social context*. Sixth Edition. New York: Oxford University Press.

Levinger, G.; Senn, D. & Jorgensen, B. (1970). Progress toward permanence in courtship: A test of the Kerckhoff-Davis hypothesis. *Sociometry, 33*, 427-433.

Mahler, M., Pine, F. & Bergman, A. (1975). *The psychological birth of the human infant: Symbiosis and individuation*. New York: Basic.

Mahler, M. (1972). On the first three subphases of the separation individuation process. *International Journal of Psychoanalysis, 53*, 333-338.

Markey, V. (1973). Psychological need relationships in dyadic attraction and rejection. *Psychological Reports, 32*, 111-123.

Mehrabian, A. (1989). Marital choice and compatibility as a function of trait similarity-dissimilarity. *Psychological Reports, 65*, 1202.

Meissner, W. (1978). The conceptualization of marriage and family dynamics from a psychoanalytic perspective. In. T. Poalino & B. McGrady (Eds.) *Marriage and marital therapy*. New York: Brunner/Mazel.

Miller, S., Nunnally, E. & Wackman, D. (1988). *Connecting with self and other*. Littleton, CO: Interpersonal Communication Programs.

Minuchin, S. (1974). *Families and family therapy*. Cambridge, MA: Harvard University Press.

Mittleman, B. (1944). Complementary neurotic reactions in intimate relationships. *The Psychoanalytic Quarterly, 13*, 479-491.

Mittleman, B. (1956). *Analysis of reciprocal neurotic patterns in family relations.* New York: Basic.

Moynihan, C. & Ingraham, B. (1971). Observing family function: Toward a definition of change. In B. Brady and C. Moynihan (Eds.) *Systems therapy.* Washington, DC: Authors.

Murstein, B. (1970). Stimulus-value-role-a theory of marital choice. *Journal of Marriage and the Family, 32*, 465-481.

Murstein, B. (1971). *Theories of attraction and love.* New York: Springer.

Murstein, B. (1976). *Who will many whom?* New York: Springer.

Murstein, B. (1986). *Paths to marriage.* CA: Sage.

Nadelson, C. (1978). Twentieth century trends in marriage and marital therapy. In T. Poalino & B. McGrady (Eds.) *Marriage and marital therapy.* New York: Brunner/Mazel.

Napier, A. (1971). The marriage of families: Cross-generational complementarity. *Family Process, 10*, 373-395.

Napier, A. (1988). *The fragile bond.* New York: Harper and Row.

Napier, A. & Whitaker, C. (1978). *The family crucible.* New York: Harper & Row.

Neill, J. & Kniskern, D. (1982). *From psyche to system: The evolving therapy of Carl Whitaker.* New York: Guilford Press.

Nichols, W. (1988). *Marital therapy: An integrative approach.* New York: Guilford Press.

Nichols, W. & Everett, C. (1986). *Systemic family therapy: An integrative approach.* New York: Guilford Press.

Ohmann, O. (1947). The psychology of attraction. In H. Jordan (Ed.) *You and marriage.* New York: Wiley.

Papp, P. (1983). *The process of change.* New York: Guilford Press.

Pascal, H. (1974). Need interaction a factor in marital adjustment. *Dissertation Abstract International, 35*, 2056-2057.

Percer, T. (1985). *Sex signals: The biology of love.* Philadelphia: ISI Press.

Phillips, K., Fulker, D., Carey, G. & Nagoshi, C. (1988). Direct marital assortment for cognitive and personality variables. *Behavior Genetics, 18*, 347-356.

Pineo, P. (1961). Disenchantment in the later years of marriage. *Marriage and Family Living, 23*, 3-11.

Poalino, T. & McGrady, B. (1978). *Marriage and marital therapy: Psychoanalytic, behavioral and systems theory perspectives.* New York: Brunner/Mazel.

Powers, E. (1971). Thirty years of research on ideal mate characteristics: What do we know? *International Journal of Sociology of the Family, 1*, 1-9.

Price, R. & Vanderberg, S. (1980). Matching for physical attractiveness in married couples. *Personality and Social Psychology Bulletin, 5*, 122-125.

Reik, T. (1957). *Of love and lust.* New York: Farrar, Strauss & Cudahy.

Reiss, I. (1960). Toward a sociology of the heterosexual love relationship. *Marriage and Family Living, 32*, 138-145.

Richardson, H. (1939). Studies of mental resemblance between husbands and wives and between friends. *Psychological Bulletin, 36*, 104-142.

Roth-Puckett, J. (1977). *The intimacy/individuation conflict: A study of the relationship between level of self-actualization and couple interaction.* Unpublished doctoral dissertation, CSPP-SF.

Rubin, Z., Kill, C., Peplau, L. & Dunkel-Schette, C. (1980). Self-disclosure in dating couple: Sex roles and the ethic of openness. *Journal of Marriage and the Family, 42*, 305-317.

Rushton, J., Russell, R. & Wells, P. (1985). Evidence for genetic similarity theory: Beyond kin selection. *Behavior Genetics, 14*, 179-193.

Sager, C. (1976). *Marital contracts and couple therapy.* New York: Brunner/Mazel.

Satir, V. (1967). *Conjoint family therapy.* Palo Alto, CA: Science and Behavior Books.

Satir, V. (1988). *The new peoplemaking.* Mountain View, CA: Science and Behavior Books.

Scarf, M. (1987). *Intimate partners: Patterns in love and marriage.* New York: Random House.

Scharf, D. & Scharf, J. (1987). *Object relations family therapy.* New York: Jason Aronson.

Schor, J. & Sanville, J. (1978). *Illusion in loving.* New York: Double Helix.

Sindberg, R. & Roberts, A. (1972). Mate selection factors in computer matched marriages. *Journal of Marriage and the Family, 34*, 611-614.

Skynner, A. (1976). *Systems of family and marital psychotherapy.* New York: Brunner/Mazel.

Slipp, S. (1984). *Object relations: A dynamic bridge between individual and family therapy.* New York: Jason Aronson.

Slipp, S. (1988). *The technique and practice of object relations family therapy.* Northvale, NJ: Jason Aronson.

Snyder, C. (1966). Marital selectivity in self-adjustment, social adjustment, and I.Q. *Journal of Marriage and the Family, 28*, 188-189.

Synder, M. & Gangestad, S. (1982). Choosing social situations: Two investigations of self-monitoring process. *Journal of Personality and Social Psychology, 43*, 123-135.

Solomon, A. (1986). Self acceptance and the selection of a marital partner: An assessment of the SVR model of Murstein. *Social, Behavior and Personality, 14*, 1-6.

Sonne, J. & Swirsky, D. (1981). Self-object considerations in marriage and marital therapy. In G. Sholevar (Ed.) *The handbook of marriage and marital therapy.* New York: SP Medical & Scientific Books.

Stuart, R. (1980). *Helping couples change.* New York: Guilford.

Szondi, L. (1937). Contributions to fate analysis, an attempt at a theory of choice in love. *Acta Psychologica, 3*, 1-80.

Thibaut, J. & Kelley, H. (1959). *The social psychology of groups.* New York: Wiley.

Toman, W. (1970). Never mind your horoscope: Birth order rules all. *Psychology Today, 4*, 45-49.

Toman, W. (1976). *Family constellation: Its effects on personality and social behavior.* New York: Springer.

Touhey, J. (1971). Birth order and mate selection. *Psychological Reports, 29*, 618.

Townsend, J. & Levy, G. (1990). Effects of potential partners' physical attractiveness and socioeconomic status on sexuality and partner choice. *Archives of Sexual Behavior, 19*, 149-164.

Trivers, R. (1972). Parental investment and sexual selection. In B. Campbell (Ed.) *Sexual selection and the descent of man.* Aldine.

Udry, R. (1965). The influence of the ideal mate image on mate selection and mate perception. *Journal of Marriage and the Family, 27*, 477-482.

U.S. Bureau of Census. (1989). Washington, DC.

Vanderberg, S. (1972). Assortive mating, or who marries whom? *Behavior Genetics, 1*, 59-71.

Ward, C.; Castro, M.; Wilcox, A. (1974). Birth order effects on mate selection and parenthood. *Journal of Social Psychology, 94*, 57-64.

Watkins, M. & Meredith, W. (1981). Spouse similarity in newlyweds with respect to specific cognitive abilities, socioeconomic status, and education. *Behavior Genetics, 11*, 1-21.

Watzlawick, P., Beavin, J. & Jackson, D. (1967). *Pragmatics of human communication.* New York: Norton.

Weinberg, L. (1978). *Differentiation and fusion in marital relations.* Unpublished doctoral dissertation, Temple University, Philadelphia.

Weininger, O. (1906). *Sex and character.* New York: Putman.

Weinrich, J. (1987). *Sexual landscapes: Why we are what we are, why we love whom we love.* New York: Scribner.

Westermarck, E. (1936). *The future of marriage in western civilization.* New York: Macmillan.

White, G. (1980). Physical attractiveness and courtship progress. *Journal of Personality and Social Psychology, 39*, 660-668.

White, S. & Hatcher, C. (1986). Couple complementarity and similarity: A review of the literature. *The American Journal of Family Therapy, 12*, 15-25.

Willi, J. (1982). *Couples in collusion.* New York: Jason Aronson.

Willi, J. (1984). *Dynamics of couples therapy.* New York: Jason Aronson.

Winch, R. (1952). *The modern family.* New York: Holt.

Winch, R. (1954). *Mate selection: A study of complementary needs.* New York: Harper & Row.

Winch, R. (1955). The theory of complementary needs in mate selection. *American Sociological Review, 20*, 552-555.

Winch, R. (1958). *Mate selection: A study of complementary needs.* Harper & Row.

Winch, R., Ktones, T., Ktones, V. (1958). Theory of complementary needs in mate selection: An analytic and descriptive study. *American Sociological Review, 19*, 241-249.

Winestone, M. (1973). The experience of separation-individuation in infancy and its reverberations through the core of life. *Journal of American Psychoanalytic Association, 21*, 135-154.

Worthy, M., Gary, A., & Kahn, G. (1969). Self-disclosure as an exchange process. *Journal of Personality and Social Psychology, 13*, 59-63.

Wynne, L. (1971). Some guidelines for exploring conjoint family therapy. In J. Haley (Ed.) *Changing families*. New York: Grune & Stratton.

Wynne, L., Ryckoff, I., Day, J., & Hirsh, S. (1958). Pseudomutuality in the family relationships of schizophrenics. *Psychiatry, 21*, 205-220.

An Overview of the Historical
and Empirical Antecedents
in the Development
of the Codependency Concept

Frank P. Troise

SUMMARY. This paper offers a general overview of the historical
and previous empirical studies leading up to the contemporary conceptualization of codependency theory. In addition the author includes a seemingly lone research attempt to examine a major personality trait universally attributed to codependents–their hypothesized
diminished capacity for intimacy.

The current concept of codependency was used to understand the
non-alcoholic spouse's behaviors and psycho-pathology in relation

---

Frank P. Troise, DSW, BCD, would like to thank Mr. Michael Aymar for his
research assistance in developing this paper.

Frank Troise June 15, 1948–May 15, 1993

Between the time of writing this article and its publication, Frank Troise
died suddenly in New York City on May 15, 1993. We regret this loss to the
mental health community–and that we will be receiving no more such
thought-filled articles from him.

Dr. Troise's brother Don, also a social worker and also a psychotherapist, is Director of the New York City Department of Health HIV Counsel-
ling and Testing Group Services Program; he requested that publication
continue as planned. Please send correspondence to: Don Troise, CSW, 146
West 86th Street, #2C, New York, NY 10024.

[Haworth co-indexing entry note]: "An Overview of the Historical and Empirical Antecedents in
the Development of the Codependency Concept," Troise, Frank P. Co-published simultaneously in the
Journal of Couples Therapy (The Haworth Press, Inc.) Vol. 4, No. 1/2, 1993, pp. 89-104; and: *Attraction
and Attachment: Understanding Styles of Relationships* (ed: Barbara Jo Brothers) The Haworth Press,
Inc., 1993, pp. 89-104. Multiple copies of this article/chapter may be purchased from The Haworth
Document Delivery Center [1-800-3-HAWORTH; 9:00 a.m. - 5:00 p.m. (EST)].

to his or her alcoholic spouse. This so-called diagnostic entity has been broadened to include, in addition, non-alcoholic relationships where the codependent selects a mate incapable of engaging in a healthy emotionally intimate relationship. Therefore a pathological interactional syndrome develops locking the codependent into certain self-defeating behaviors which are psychogenetically connected to, and resonate with, the codependent's dysfunctional family of origin. This paper focuses primarily on women, or codependents, who are married to alcoholics.

INTRODUCTION

Despite the fact that codependency theory is a widely accepted diagnostic entity in both the mental health and lay population its validity has not been supported by empirical research (Kokin and Walker, 1989). Cermak (1986) has argued for its inclusion in the diagnostic and statistical manual. Others (Black, 1982; Subby, 1987; Wegsheider-Cruse, 1985;) have written self-help books on the subject, developed treatment centers for codependency and lectured extensively on the pervasiveness of codependency in contemporary culture. Furthermore, prior empirical studies (Bailey, 1967; Jackson, 1954; Haberman, 1964), crucial to the development of Codependency Theory, are conspicuously absent in the literature with the exception of Kokin and Walker's (1989) criticism of Codependency Theory as it relates to wives of alcoholics. Despite the absence or use of prior or present research codependency has been legitimized as a valid diagnostic entity, supposedly characterized by identifiable behaviors and interactional pathological syndromes which are perpetuated by the codependent in a marriage to an alcoholic. While the contemporary definition of codependency includes both males and females, a review of the literature (Kokin and Walker, 1989) strongly suggests that women are the predominate bearers of this psychological condition. Their own psychogenetically grounded "neurotic" predisposition to select floridly symptomatic spouses makes them "enablers" (Subby, 1987) who are both "volunteers" and "victims" of their alcoholic spouses' illness. Their "enabling" behavior perpetuates their spouses' alcoholism and locks them into a pathological interactional syndrome which prohibits a healthy marriage. Simply stated, such wives, or codependents, enter the marriage to the alcoholic with a pre-existing psychopathology. Such a marriage is both painful to the codependent yet pathologically gratifying given its familiarity and resonance with her disturbed prior involvement with a "dysfunctional family" of origin. Clearly, Codependency Theory strongly suggests psychological investment on the part of the codependent in her husband's illness. She is, therefore, a "volunteer-victim" both suffering from her husband's alcoholism yet exploiting it for psychopathologic secondary gain. This basic etiologic and psychodynamic conceptualization of codependency is consistent with previous psychoanalytically informed theories, developed in the 1950's, which were defined as the "Disturbed Personality Theory" (Futterman, 1953; McDonald, 1956; Price, 1945) of wives of alcoholics. These psychoanalytic formulations inferred that the married alcoholic's personality and drinking problems were intimately related to the pathologic need and security operations of the non-alcoholic spouse.

An overview of the "Disturbed Personality Theory" will be presented following a general summary of Codependency Theory. The paper will then trace the empirical challenges to the "Disturbed Personality Theory" to include a feminist historical perspective on the sociological climate in which this theory developed. Finally the author will conclude with a seemingly lone empirical study (Troise, 1992) examining a primary personality characteristic attributed to codependents–that is, the diminished capacity for experiencing intimacy amongst wives of alcoholics or codependents.

CONTEMPORARY CODEPENDENCY THEORY

Kokin and Walker (1989) have noted that the contemporary description of codependents is so broad that it is almost indistinguishable from other personality disorders or pathological interactional syndromes. Some theorists (Black, 1982; Larsen, 1985; Subby, 1987) stress etiological factors which interact with the conflict and stress generated by the alcoholic spouse. Others, while recognizing etiological contributions grounded in the codependent's dysfunctional family of origin, focus on her maladaptive reactions to living with an alcoholic (Wegsheider-Cruse, 1985). Given the wide range of characteristics attributed to codependents the author has selected those behaviors and interactional syndromes agreed upon by most codependency theorists. Again, these pathologic configurations supposedly distinguish codependents from other diagnostic entities and contribute to the codependent's selection of an alcoholic or pre-alcoholic mate, the perpetuation of the spouses' alcoholism and the disturbed interaction between the codependent and the alcoholic spouse.

Larsen (1985) states that codependency is characterized by those self-defeating learned behaviors or character defects that result in an incapacity to initiate or to participate in loving relationships. In this view the codependent seeks out a troubled person (i.e., alcoholic) for a mate since this relationship defends the codependent against intrapsychic conflicts concerning intimacy which resonate with their dysfunctional family of origin. These behaviors, or coping mechanisms, would prevail throughout the codependent's life and permeate significant relationships (Beattie, 1987). Generally stated these characteristics are as follows: Codependents tend to come from dysfunctional families, suffer from a lack of self worth and have major difficulties in establishing and experiencing intimate relationships. The interpersonal boundaries in their relationships are fluid and characterized by their attempts at controlling the object and denying their partners' problems. They lack trust and are typically dependent. Codependents find it hard to express their emotions and repress their anger. These characteristics organize primarily around interpersonal interaction. The common link amongst codependents is more readily detected in their maladaptive behavioral patterns within the context of significant relationships which require a mature capacity for intimacy.

THE "DISTURBED PERSONALITY" THEORY

The theory of "Disturbed Personality" was the first postulated to account for psychological disturbance seen in wives of alcoholics during the first half of this century (Edwards, Harvey, Whitehead, 1972).

As previously mentioned psychoanalytic social workers and psychiatrists (Bailey and Haberman, 1962; Ballard, 1959; Clifford, 1960; Futterman, 1953; McDonald, 1956; Rae and Forbes, 1966) suggested that women with certain personality types tend to select alcoholics or potential alcoholics as mates in order to satisfy unconscious needs of their own. These needs supposedly foster the continued drinking of the husband.

In one of the first articles devoted to such women, Lewis (1937) described them as having found an outlet for their own anger in their relationships with men who were dependent on them and who created situations which forced the wives to 'punish' their husbands. Boggs (1944) found that some wives fought their husband's attempts to get help, which undermined the treatment and kept the husband ineffectual. He theorized that this behavior was a means of justifying their own continued hostility and of camouflaging their inadequacies and inner conflicts.

In his observational study of the wives of twenty alcoholics, Price (1945) described the women as typically dependent persons who had become hostile upon finding that their husbands were too dependent. The women in this study often interpreted their husbands' drinking as a rejection of their dependency needs. To 'get even,' Price's subjects became more demanding or assumed inordinate responsibility in their marriages making their husbands feel even more inadequate. Price also observed that these wives would usually fight treatment unconsciously. He concluded that they "needed" the husband to be alcoholic as proof of their own superiority and their husbands' inferiority.

Whalen (1953) described wives of alcoholics, she saw in a family service agency, as having married these men to fulfill certain personality needs of their own and because their husbands possessed certain personality deficiencies that met these needs. She identified 'types' among the wives, including 'martyrs,' 'punishers,' 'controllers' and 'needers.' Whalen (1953), by attempting to identify certain types among women who chose alcoholic husbands because of their own personality needs, and Price (1945), by noting their dependence, foreshadowed some of the work currently called "Codependency" Theory.

Futterman (1953) concluded, from clinical observation, that wives of alcoholics, because of their own needs, seemed unconsciously to encourage their husbands' alcoholism. He theorized that because of their strong identification with a dominant mother they felt unconsciously inadequate and so chose a weak, dependent husband. He believed that when this symbiotic relationship was disturbed, by the husband's attempt to recover, the wife would 'decompensate.' That is, her personality would deteriorate with the loosening of pre-existing psychological defenses resulting in an increase in affective symptoms (i.e., depression and anxiety) and decreased ability to function adequately. Some wives developed psychosomatic illness during their husband's recovery period.

McDonald (1956) examined Futterman's notion of decompensation among eighteen patients of a state psychiatric hospital whose husbands were alcoholics. He found eleven cases of decompensation connected to an improvement in the husband's condition, one associated with worsening alcoholism, and six in which there was no change in the husband's drinking patterns. McDonald noted that although a number of the patients had diagnosable personality disorders, they had shown no signs of deterioration until their husband's drinking patterns changed for the better.

While these pioneering studies were based primarily on clinical observation, McDonald did find evidence that suggested that a significant number of wives of alcoholics were, in some way, psychologically invested in the maintenance of their husband's alcoholism. His work confirmed, to some degree, Futterman's hypothesis that many wives of alcoholics would psychologically decompensate when the alcoholic spouse recovered.

THE "DISTURBED PERSONALITY THEORY": A FEMINIST PERSPECTIVE

During World War II the nation applauded women for their participation in the national war effort. However, this applause rapidly turned to criticism of women for having gone to work during the war and thereby destroying the American family in the process. Men returned from war and women were now defined as having given up their femininity and maternal role to compete with men causing their children to become delinquents and their husbands to become alcoholics (Banner, 1974).

Freudianism, according to Banner, had begun to have a major influence on American psychiatry and psychiatric social work practice. As previously noted, it was Freudian psychiatrists and psychoanalytic social workers who developed the "Disturbed Personality Theory." They argued that women could attain emotional stability only through domesticity and motherhood. Thus, women who now worked denied their natural needs and threatened the family structure. This bitter anti-feminism of the immediate post-war years echoed throughout the 1950's, forming a body of thought that influenced sociologists, psychoanalysts, school teachers, etc., in a way that clearly blamed women for the psychopathology of the returning male draftees and the increase in alcoholism amongst male war veterans. The "Disturbed Personality Theory" was born within this social context and was heavily influenced by Freudian psychology which defined women's burgeoning work identity and independence as competitive and castrating towards men. Banner concludes that such theories were a reaction to the threat that female independence posed to men. Freudian psychology reinforced the idea that such autonomy in women was designed unconsciously to psychologically castrate men, rendering them susceptible to alcoholism and covertly encouraging or perpetuating their illness for the neurotic needs of the non-alcoholic spouses.

THE "STRESS" THEORY

The "stress" or "reaction to stress" theory (Edwards et al., 1972) developed as more and more social welfare agencies and counselors began to take on the problems of the family as a unit where one or both spouses were alcoholic.

An increased understanding of family systems theory in the 1950's, and a desire to test the psychoanalytic observations generated by the "Disturbed Personality Theory" further prompted empirical study which formed the basis for the "Stress Theory."

Jackson and Kogan (1954) were the first to hypothesize that the neurotic traits, affective symptoms and psychosocial disturbances, commonly detected in the wives of alcoholics, were a reaction to the stress of living with an alcoholic and the marital and family conflict that the alcoholic provoked by his behavior. For example, the "stress theory" suggests that commonly observed uncooperative or dominant behavior on the part of the wife was a coping mechanism developed to maintain family functioning and stability.

Likewise, the wife's tendency to ignore changes in her husband's behavior (i.e., recovery) and retain the same aforementioned "coping" strategies were not a result of her pathological needs but a realistic recognition of the husband's undependability (Jackson and Kogan, 1954). In this view the wife's increased symptomatology during the husband's recovery was merely a continued reaction to the impending threat that the alcoholic could relapse at any given time. Therefore the wife, in this situation, maintained previous defenses in an attempt to prepare for the "inevitable" relapse.

In Jackson and Kogan's study (1954) the "stress" hypothesis was tested by comparing spouses whose husbands were abstinent (but who had been heavy drinkers) with spouses of currently heavy drinking alcoholics. They compared the MMPI (Minnesota Multiphasic Personality Inventory) scores of twenty-six wives of recovering alcoholics with those of fifty wives of active alcoholics and fifty wives of non-alcoholics. Wives of non-alcoholics had the lowest rate of personality disturbance, wives of actively drinking alcoholics had the highest rate and wives of recovered or inactive alcoholics were in-between.

Bailey (1967) and Haberman (1964) found that women whose husbands were abstinent (although problem drinking had occurred earlier in the marriage) reported fewer psychophysiological symptoms (i.e., gastrointestinal problems) than women whose husbands were currently drinking. Paolino and McCrady (1977) noted that spouses of alcoholics in treatment showed significant decreases in anxiety and depression as their partners' drinking problems improved. "Stress" theorists felt that these studies supported the "reaction to stress" hypothesis and disproved the "Disturbed Personality Theory" since wives of abstinent alcoholics (who should be under less stress) were less "impaired" than wives of active alcoholics.

Bailey, Haberman and Alksne (1962) attempted to examine both "Disturbed Personality Theory" and "Stress Theories" as to whether the disturbance observed in wives of alcoholics antedates the marriage or stems from the cumulative stresses of the husband's progressive illness. Since the wife is assumed to play a primary role in the course of the alcoholics' illness and in his motivation to recover, the divergent theoretical approaches were examined by Bailey et al. by comparing groups of women whose marriages to alcoholics have had different outcomes: divorce, recovery of the husband, or maintenance of the marriage with an actively drinking spouse.

In order to determine the degree of psychological disturbance in the wives in all three groups structured interviews were conducted. The interviews included twenty-two questions in psychophysiological and psychoneurotic symptoms extracted from the United States Army Neuropsychiatric Screening Adjunct and Minnesota Multiphasic Personality Inventory. If it were true, according to the "Disturbed Personality Theory," that the wives' psychological disturbance antedates the marriage to the alcoholic, and that these women needed the alcoholic to drink in order to maintain their own psychological equilibrium, then it would be expected that they would suffer an increase in symptoms once the marriage ended or the husband recovered. If the "stress" theory were valid then these wives would be expected to experience significantly less psychological disturbance once the marriage was terminated or the husband was recovering. This group was compared to wives who remained in marriages with actively drinking alcoholics.

The results revealed that the separated or divorced wives believed they had improved after ending the marriage. Those wives whose husbands achieved sobriety during the marriage saw themselves as improved even more markedly than the separated or divorced group. It was not possible to determine changes in the scores of wives of actively drinking husbands since few of them could remember a clear contrast period. That is, an earlier time during the marriage when they had not been exposed to their husband's drinking.

Historically, the quantitative and qualitative empirical research of the proponents of the "Stress Theory" was accepted. The "Disturbed Personality Theory" was, for the most part, abandoned in favor of the belief that wives of alcoholics were no different in their psychological distress or personality disturbance, then any other wives who were experiencing marital distress or conflict. The theory that wives of alcoholics had a common unitary personality disturbance, that underscored their involvement and investment in the alcoholic spouses' illness, was abandoned by most mental health professionals by the late 1960's (Edwards et al., 1972).

EMPIRICAL STUDY OF THE CAPACITY FOR INTIMACY IN WIVES OF ALCOHOLICS OR CODEPENDENTS

The codependent's pre-existing diminished capacity for experiencing intimacy is central to the psychodynamic and interactional psychopathology typically ascribed to this population. This primary organizing personality deficit, which supposedly antedates the marriage to the alcoholic, is viewed by Codependency Theorists (Black, 1982; Subby, 1987; Wegsheider-Cruse, 1985), as a primary contributor in the disturbed interactional pattern and "enabling" behavior which perpetuates the alcoholic's continued drinking. Simply stated the codependent unconsciously needs the alcoholic to drink because the conflict generated by the alcoholic protects the codependent from a feared emotionally intimate relationship. This lack of intimacy and marital conflict, while painful, is familiar and safe for the codependent given its resonance with disturbed interactional patterns in her family of origin.

Given the primacy of the codependent's hypothesized impaired capacity for experiencing intimacy, in any significant relationship, it is reasonable to assume that such an impairment would be evident in the codependent's relationship with her "best" or "closest" friend. An empirical study was conducted (Troise, 1991) in which an experimental group (n = 120) of wives of alcoholics or codependents were compared to a control group of wives of non-alcoholics (n = 120) measuring the difference in the subjects' capacity for experiencing intimacy. Both groups were asked to complete the Miller Social Intimacy Scale (Miller and Lefcourt, 1982) as it pertains to their experience of emotional intimacy in their relationship to their "best" or "closest" friend. The hypothesis predicted that the codependents would score significantly lower in their capacity to experience intimacy in their relationship with their closest friend when compared to controls.

There were no significant differences between the mean scores of the codependents and the controls in their experience of emotional intimacy with their respective "best" or "closest" friends. It is important to note that the sample was stratified for adult children of alcoholics. The hypothesis was not proven thereby offering some support for the "reaction to stress" theorists' findings which suggested that there was no unitary personality configuration or psychological disturbance which distinguishes wives of alcoholics or codependents from other wives. Interestingly enough this empirical study stands alone in the literature on Codependency Theory which is primarily grounded in observations in clinical practice. Furthermore the codependency literature is conspicuously lacking in reference to previous empirical studies ("Stress Theory") which were unable to link wives of alcoholics together vis-à-vis a common personality disturbance or traits.

DISCUSSION

This historical overview of the research which foreshadowed the development of contemporary Codependency Theory reveals that the basic theoretical construct, which informs Codependency Theory, was abandoned by mental health researchers in the late 1950's and early 1960's. Attempts to link wives of alcoholics together with a shared personality disturbance, which contributed to their selection of an alcoholic mate and the perpetuation of the alcoholic's illness, were put to rest by the findings of the "Reaction to Stress" theorists. Furthermore, history reveals that the original "Disturbed Personality Theory" of wives of alcoholics, which clearly shares a similar theoretical foundation with contemporary Codependency Theory, was intimately connected to long since abandoned Freudian concepts regarding innate masochism in women. In addition Banner (1974) has noted that this theory was developed within a social climate which blamed the assertiveness of women for the psychological difficulties of men returning from World War II.

Most codependency theorists attribute the codependent's behavior to a combination of failed coping attempts in dealing with the alcoholic's destructive behavior and a pre-existing psychopathology which attracts the codependent to a disturbed relationship thereby perpetuating and exploiting it for psychopathologic gain (i.e., repetition compulsion). Nevertheless the notion of codependents as "enablers" in their symptomatic spouses' illness, strongly suggests a blaming of the victim who is married to someone who is creating havoc in the marriage due to his alcoholism.

Bowen (1978) has noted that the symptoms of one spouse may be needed by the other mate in order to mask or defend the non-symptomatic spouse against personality deficits. In such an instance the symptomatic spouses' illness is needed to maintain homeostasis in the relationship. Merikangas (1982) found that individuals who are symptomatic but have a vulnerability to develop a psychiatric disorder (i.e., alcoholism) and therefore display behavioral anomalies, withdrawal, and a lack of social skills are less likely to develop mature intimate healthy relationships. Consequently, these individuals are either selected out of the "marital pool" or marry individuals who are similarly impaired. Clinical observation of married couples in conflict often reveal that the florid symptoms of one spouse are needed and exploited for psychopathologic gain by the non-symptomatic spouse. However the widespread acceptance of codependency as a distinguishable diagnostic entity, without the benefit of empirical validation or recognition of previously related research, encourages pre-conceived sweeping notions regarding women who marry alcoholics by mental health professionals.

Kokin and Walker (1989) have stated that the concept of codependency is firmly grounded in antiquated and empirically unfounded Freudian beliefs that women enjoy their suffering based on innate biologically grounded masochistic tendencies. They argue that expert professionals find it difficult to diagnose and treat alcoholism yet when the wife of the alcoholic or codependent flounders in dealing with her alcoholic spouse she is accused of perpetuating his illness for psychopathologic gain. They further state that believing that women are codependents takes the focus off the alcoholic himself and provides some relief since alcoholism is so difficult to treat and recovery rate is so low. Furthermore it encourages the blaming of women for yet another problem. Women-blaming in our culture is a widely accepted activity as it was in the 1940's and 1950's when the related disturbed "Personalty Theory" was born. Interestingly enough both time periods were characterized by increased female independence and demands for equal status with men. Kokin and Walker suggest that Codependency Theory has created a whole new set of jargon and counterintuitive principles giving bewildered and frustrated professionals a sense of control, power and efficacy as they now speak a new language that lay people cannot understand. Lastly the non-alcoholic spouse, or code-pendent, is eminently more treatable, and in many cases quite will-ing to assume blame or personality disturbance in a marriage to an alcoholic. In such an instance the alcoholism clinician can more easily experience some measure of success in treatment of the code-pendent as opposed to regular treatment failures with the alcoholic spouse. The patient who defines herself as "enabler" or a contribu-tor to her failing marriage, based on her own codependent personal-ity disorder, maintains and perpetuates the illusion that she can have some influence over her husband's alcoholism vis-à-vis treatment for her codependency.

In summary, a historical overview of the empirical research and theories regarding wives of alcoholics, which foreshadowed the development of Codependency Theory, strongly suggests the need for integration of prior research and the empirical study of contem-porary Codependency Theory. Sweeping acceptance of this theory, by both mental health and the lay population, has proceeded with-out the benefit of coordinated empirical research.

Undoubtedly there are those patients who suffer from psycho-pathology, consistent with codependence. Others inadvertently en-ter marriage to an alcoholic and become victims of the stress and conflict generated by the alcoholic's destructive behavior. Prior research, conspicuously absent in contemporary codependency lit-erature, has failed to provide convincing evidence that wives of alcoholics or codependents share any unitary personality configura-tion–healthy or pathological. Premature acceptance of this theory and diagnostic entity seriously influence and limit the mental health clinician's understanding and treatment of a population that has already been traumatized, confused, blamed and misunderstood given the chaotic nature of the alcoholic marriage. To ascribe cer-tain personality deficits as contributing factors which "enable" or perpetuate the alcoholic's illness to wives of alcoholics amounts to perpetuating the blame of such wives for their husbands' disease. It further perpetuates the illusion that the wife, were she to alter her "enabling" behavior, would then have some significant impact on her husband's alcoholism.

Some attempts by wives of alcoholics or codependents to cope with the disturbance generated by their alcoholic spouse inadvertently allow the alcoholic to continue drinking. Many wives are not familiar with the alcoholic syndrome and unknowingly support the alcoholic's denial through various attempts to maintain marriage, family and social or employment obligations. Such attempts often prolong the alcoholic's recognition of the erosive effects that alcoholism is having on his family, marriage, social and employment life. However, to define the wife's attempts at coping with such an unfamiliar mental health problem as pathologically gratifying obfuscates the essence of the difficulty the non-alcoholic spouse is having in coping with such a marital trauma. Given the almost all inclusive diagnostic picture attributed to codependents and the willingness of many wives of alcoholics to assume some blame for their husbands' alcoholism many so-called codependents will readily conform to and accept a codependent diagnosis. Kokin and Walker offer a simple yet profound example of the basic adaptive function of the codependent in dealing with the alcoholic's destructive behavior. They say that if the codependent assumes responsibility for driving an automobile, with children in it, because the husband is too drunk to drive she is merely protecting her family from potential disaster. While this example is somewhat obvious it is metaphorically significant in terms of the so-called "enabling" behaviors attributed to codependents. The psychopathology or "enabling" behavior of the wife of the alcoholic, so defined by codependency theory, is more often than not the only option available to a wife who *must* assume responsibility for her and her family's welfare given her alcoholic husband's inability to do so. While such behavior may inadvertently perpetuate the alcoholic's disease it must be, at first, considered as an attempt to legitimately and reasonably cope with the trauma imposed on her by her alcoholic husband.

Clinical wisdom suggests that certain interactions between floridly symptomatic spouses and their "non-symptomatic" partners are often perpetuated and exploited for psychopathologic gain by the "non-symptomatic" spouse. Codependency Theory, however, returns full circle to a theory, previously abandoned through empirical research, which obliterates differential diagnosis, ignores the impact of reality trauma of alcoholism on the non-alcoholic spouse and is seemingly a thinly disguised version of previously abandoned Freudian concepts which blame women for the difficulties of men. Further empirical study of contemporary Codependency Theory along with integration of prior empirical studies, which foreshadow the development of Codependency Theory, are needed before mental health professionals and the lay population accept this theory as if it is a valid diagnostic entity.

BIBLIOGRAPHY

Bailey, M.B., Haberman, P. and Alksne, H. (1962). Outcomes of alcoholic marriages; endurance, termination or recovery. *Quart. J. Stud. Alc.* 23: 610-623, (CAAL, 9584).

Bailey, M.B. (1967). Psychophysiological impairment in wives of alcoholics as related to their husbands' drinking and sobriety. Pp. 134-144. In: Fox, R., (ed.), *Alcoholism, behavioral research, therapeutic approaches.* New York: Springer.

Ballard, R. G. (1959). The interrelatedness of alcoholism and marital conflict symposium: 3. The interaction between marital conflict and alcoholism as seen through MMPI's of marriage partners. *American Journal of Orthopsychiatry, 29,* 528-546.

Banner, L.W. (1974). *Women in modern america: A brief history.* Harcourt, Brace and Jovanovich, 2nd Edition.

Beattie, M. (1987). *Codependent no more.* New York: Harper and Row.

Black, C. (1982). *It will never happen to me.* Denver: M.A.C.

Boggs, M. H. (1944). The role of social work in the treatment of inebriates. *Quarterly Journal of Studies on Alcohol, 4,* 557-567.

Bowen, M. (1978). *Family therapy and clinical practice.* New York/London: Jason Aronson, Inc.

Cermak, T. L. (1986). *Diagnosing and treating codependence.* Minneapolis: Johnson Institute.

Clifford, B. J. (1960). A study of the wives of rehabilitated and unrehabilitated alcoholics. *Social Casework, 41,* 457-460.

Edwards, P., Harvey, C., & Whitehead, P. C. (1972). Wives of alcoholics: A critical review and analysis. *Quarterly Journal of Studies on Alcohol, 34,* 112-132.

Futterman, S. (1953). Personality trends in wives of alcoholics. *Journal of Psychiatric Social Work, 23,* 37-41.

Haberman, P.W. (1964) Psychological test score changes for wives of alcoholics during periods of drinking and sobriety. *J. Clin. Psychol.* 20: 230-232, (CAAAL, 10418).

Jackson, J. K. (1954). The adjustment of the family to the crisis of alcoholism. *Quarterly Journal of Studies on Alcohol, 15,* 562-586.

Kokin, M. and Walker, I. (1989). *Women married to alcoholics.* New York: William Morrow and Company, Inc.

Larsen, E. (1985). "Codependency Seminar," Stillwater, MN.

Lewis, M. F. (1937). Alcoholism and family casework. *Family, 18,* 39-44.

Lewis, M. L. (1954). The initial contact with wives of alcoholics. *Social Casework, 35,* 8-13.

McDonald, D. E. (1956). Mental disorders in wives of alcoholics. *Quarterly Journal of Studies on Alcohol, 17,* 282-287.

Merikangas, K. R. (1982). *Assortative Mating for Psychiatric Disorders and Psychological Traits.* Archives of General Psychiatry.

Miller, R.S., and Lefcourt, H.M. (1982). The assessment of social intimacy. *Journal of Personality Assessment, 46* (5), 514-518.

Paolino, T. J., Jr., & McCrady, B. S. (1977). *The alcoholic marriage: Alternative perspectives.* New York: Grune & Stratton.

Price, J. M. (1945). A study of the wives of twenty alcoholics. *Quarterly Journal of Studies on Alcohol, 5,* 620-627.

Rae, J.B. and Forbes, A.R. (1966). Clinical and psychometric characteristics of wives of alcoholics. *Brit. J. Psychiat.* 112; 197-200.

Subby, R. (1987). *Lost in the shuffle.* Pompano Beach, FL: Health Communications.

Troise, F. P. (1991). "The Capacity For Intimacy in Wives of Alcoholics." Unpublished dissertation. Adelphi University School of Social Work, Garden City, New York.

Wegsheider-Cruse, S. (1985). *Choice-Making.* Pompano Beach, FL: Health Communications.

Whalen, T. (1953). Wives of alcoholics: Four types observed in a family service agency. *Quarterly Journal of Studies on Alcohol, 14,* 623-641.

Codependency and Depression:
A Correlational Study

Betsey Backe
Erin L. Bonck
Marie L. Riley

SUMMARY. The focus of this study was to investigate a correlation between codependency and depression. The instruments that were used for the study were the Beck Depression Inventory (BDI) and The Awareness Activity: How Codependent Are You? Results of this study were based on 149 paired inventories. The individuals who volunteered to complete the inventories were selected from three clinical settings in the New Orleans area. Subjects utilized were adults of both sexes and all ages. There was a strong, positive correlation between the two variables, codependency and depression, of .5966 (p < .00001). When the relationship between codependency and depression was assessed for each of the separate groups, the same trend prevailed across all three groups.

While one cannot conclude from this study that codependency and depression are equal, one may suggest that a relationship exists between them. These findings indicate that if a person reports himself/herself to be highly codependent, he/she is likely to experience an elevated level of depression.

Betsey Backe, MS, MSW, is Director of the Divorce Center in Slidell and New Orleans, LA.

Erin L. Bonck, MSW, is Director of Social Services and Field Operations for Metro Home Health Care, Inc. in Marrero, LA.

Marie L. Riley, RN, LMSW, is affiliated with Clayton Country Mental Health Center in Jonesboro, GA.

[Haworth co-indexing entry note]: "Codependency and Depression: A Correlational Study," Backe, Betsey, Erin L. Bonck, and Marie L. Riley. Co-published simultaneously in the *Journal of Couples Therapy* (The Haworth Press, Inc.) Vol. 4, No. 1/2, 1993, pp. 105-127; and: *Attraction and Attachment: Understanding Styles of Relationships* (ed: Barbara Jo Brothers) The Haworth Press, Inc., 1993, pp. 105-127. Multiple copies of this article/chapter may be purchased from The Haworth Document Delivery Center [1-800-3-HAWORTH; 9:00 a.m. - 5:00 p.m. (EST)].

105

This correlational study attempted to identify if a relationship exists between codependency and depression. Furthermore, this study attempted to give empirical legitimacy to a codependency inventory, The Awareness Activity: How Codependent Are You? (also referred to in this paper as the codependency inventory). For the purpose of this paper, codependency is defined as an emotional, psychological, and behavioral condition that manifests itself in exaggerated dependency and the extreme need for external validation which results in a loss of a sense of self (Cermak, 1986). Depression is defined as a multifaceted syndrome that features a disturbance of mood and manifests itself in such symptoms as hopelessness, helplessness, and self depreciation (Millon & Kotik, 1985).

The instruments that were used for the study were the Beck Depression Inventory (BDI) and The Awareness Activity: How Codependent Are You? (see Appendix A). Although the BDI is well established, the Awareness Activity that was used to assess codependency had not been established empirically. Therefore, this study was also a further reliability and validity test of The Awareness Activity: How Codependent Are You?

For this study the hypothesis was made that there would be a positive correlation between a measure of depression and a measure of codependency. In addition, a second hypothesis was made that women would show a higher statistically significant degree of codependency than men.

Codependency has become a trendy psychological label used to describe or characterize dysfunctional interpersonal relationships. The ever-growing popularity of this emerging concept has warranted an attempt on the part of some professionals to develop an understanding of the dynamics involved in codependency. Depression, on the other hand, is a concept that has been exhaustively researched with ever-increasing progress towards assessment, diagnosis, and treatment. Little consensus exists concerning depression and codependency theory or application. J. K. Wing and P. Bebbington (1985) suggest that problems arise in study of any disorder where there is disagreement regarding criteria for definition, and that any associations found can only provide clues of hypotheses as to the direction of cause and effect. Therefore, in order to begin developing hypotheses on codependency, researchers must establish a generally agreed upon criteria for definition. Warner Mendenhall (1989) proposes that healthcare professionals need to choose a vocabulary that facilitates communication among each other while also meeting the needs of the patient. Once a vocabulary delineating the criteria of codependency has been established, professionals must empirically test the variables contained in the criteria. In an attempt to clarify the dynamics of codependency, many authors have contributed by formulating definitions.

In his article, "Inside the Chemically Dependent Marriage: Denial and Manipulation," Robert Subby (1984) identifies codependency as "an emotional, psychological, and behavioral condition that develops as a result of an individual's prolonged exposure to, and practice of, a set of oppressive rules—rules which prevent the open expression of feeling as well as the direct discussion of personal and interpersonal problems" (p. 26). The rigidity of this set of rules traps the individual into a dysfunctional spiral of coping and problem solving which is maintained within and outside of the family system. As a result, family members interact with each other and with others by portraying their false selves rather that freely revealing their true selves.

Sharon Wegscheider-Cruse (1985), in *Choicemaking*, defines codependency as "a specific condition that is characterized by preoccupation and extreme dependence (emotionally, socially, and sometimes physically) on a person or object" (p. 2) which eventually becomes pathological in all relationships. Similar to Subby, Wegscheider-Cruse contends that this learned behavioral response will be maintained within and outside of the precipitating system.

Sondra Smalley and J.C. Coleman (1987), in their article, "Treating Intimacy Dysfunctions in Dyadic Relationships among Chemically Dependent and Codependent Clients," prescribe that codependency is "an easily identifiable (overt) or carefully disguised (covert) learned pattern of exaggerated dependency and extreme and painful external validation, with resulting identity confusion" (p. 231). Furthermore, the authors believe that codependency is a set of learned patterns (emotional, attitudinal, and behavioral) that can be either personality traits or personality disorders.

Mendenhall (1989), as mentioned earlier, stresses the importance of agreement of terms in the vocabulary of alcoholism/codependency as a result of the already existing myths and misconceptions surrounding this subject. He asserts that family members develop problems in response to the behavior of the alcoholic, not in response to the disease itself. Therefore, Mendenhall defines codependency as a condition that results from the stress of being in a relationship with an alcoholic or addict. Consequently, this stress permanently depletes a person's ability to adapt.

Ronald and Patricia Potter-Efron (1989), in their article, "Assessment of Codependency with Individuals from Alcoholic and Chemically Dependent Families," defines a codependent as "someone who has been significantly affected in specific ways by current or past involvement in an alcoholic, chemically dependent or other long term highly stressful family environment. Specific effects include: (a) fear; (b) shame/guilt; (c) prolonged despair; (d) anger; (e) denial; (f) rigidity; (g) impaired identity development; (h) confusion" (p. 39).

Inclusive of the above mentioned definitions and others, Charles L. Whitfield (1989) has developed his own definition of codependency. Whitfield perceives codependency "as a disease of lost selfhood," or more specifically, "as any suffering and/or dysfunction that is associated with or results from focusing on the needs and behavior of others" (p. 19). The historical background of codependency is most closely related to earlier descriptions of dependent personality traits or disorders. In her book, *Neurosis in Human Understanding*, Karen Horney (1950) describes dependency similarly to codependency. Horney asserts that healthy adults are capable of autonomous functioning while depending on the physical and emotional presence, support, and caring of others. This interdependence promotes personal growth and the realization of individuality. Similar to codependency, according to Horney, neurosis would result if an individual relied too heavily on others for self-fulfillment. As a result of not being able to provide reliable or valid support for her description of dependent personality traits or disorders, her insightful ideas were not influential with either the public or with other professionals.

When examining codependency, Margit K. Epstein and Eugene K. Epstein (1990), in their article, "Codependence as Social Narrative," view this concept from a systems perspective considering the "current social, political, and cultural narratives" (p. 7). Furthermore, Epstein and Epstein suggest that prevailing cultural messages must be taken into consideration when examining causality and treatment. Hence, the concept of codependency must be explored within the context of person-in-environment. Women have been socialized to be nurturers and caretakers within our culture. A description of codependency includes obtaining one's own sense of self from nurturing and caring for others. Epstein and Epstein go on to state that "It is not surprising, then, that the population defined as being codependent is made up primarily of women" (p. 6).

In his book, *Disorders of Personality*, Theodore Millon (1981) devised diagnostic criteria to provide an explanation of dependent personalities on human behavior. He distinguished Dependent Personality Disorder as a pattern of behavior in which the individual passively allows others to take full responsibility for significant life activities. Furthermore, as a result of not having the self-confidence to function independently, the dependent person adopts a helpless/ hopeless identity. Although similarities exist between dependent personality traits and disorders, Timmen L. Cermak (1986) has devised diagnostic criteria for codependent personality traits and disorders in order to provide clarity for this confusing term.

Cermak (1986) attributes confusion around the term codependency to not having an integrated definition that equals other diagnostic categories in *The Diagnostic Statistical Manual Third Edition* (DSM III) and to the lack of empirical evidence. Each of these two factors are important to accurately assess, diagnose and treat codependent persons.

> Without such criteria, no standards exist for assessing the presence and depth of pathology, for developing appropriate treatment plans, or for evaluating the effectiveness of therapy. Treatment team members are hindered in their efforts to communicate clearly and understandably about specific patient, and comparison studies of codependence are not possible. Unless we can begin gathering reliable and valid research data, codependence will remain confined to clinical impression and anecdote. (Cermak, 1986, p. 3)

The diagnostic criteria that Cermak (1986) identified was developed with the intention of providing an explanation of human behavior in order to help alleviate the physical, emotional, and intrapsychic suffering that results from dysfunctional interpersonal relations. Cermak (1986) lists the essential features of codependency as follows:

(a) continual investment of self-esteem in the ability to influence/control feelings and behavior in self and others in the face of obvious adverse consequences; (b) assumption of responsibility for meeting other's needs to the exclusion of acknowledging one's own needs; (c) anxiety and boundary distortions, in situations of intimacy and separation; (d) enmeshment in relationships with personality disordered, drug-dependent and impulse disordered individuals; and (e) exhibits–in any combination of three or more: (1) excessive reliance on denial; (2) constriction of emotions with or without dramatic outbursts; (3) depression; (4) hypervigilance; (5) compulsions; (6) anxiety; (7) substance abuse; (8) recurrent physical or sexual abuse; (9) stress-related medical illnesses; and/or (10) a primary relationship with an active substance abuser for at least two years without seeking outside help. (p. 11)

As mentioned earlier, the concept of depression has been rigorously studied resulting in various avenues to explore the possible causes, associations, and dynamics. Brian F. Shaw, T. Michael Vallis and Scott B. McCabe (1985) discern that depression is an ubiquitous term that has been used in a variety of ways. As a result, Shaw et al. (1985) indicate that from a clinical perspective it is important to differentiate conditions where the symptoms of depression are concomitants of another disorder rather than a primary diagnosis. Therefore, the coexistence of depression with other disorders as well as respective models of depression must be examined.

Theodore Millon and Doreen Kotik (1985), in their article, "The Relationship of Depression to Disorders of Personality," suggest the possibility that personality patterns are etiological and, thus, are formed before the onset of depression. Therefore, personality patterns establish the susceptibility for the development of depressive symptoms. Depending on the premorbid personality, depressive symptoms, such as hopelessness, helplessness, and self-deprecation, may induce secondary gains. For example, Millon and Kotik (1985) define secondary gains as eliciting nurturance from others, avoiding unwanted responsibilities, rationalizing poor performance, or as a method for safely expressing anger towards others.

Of the personality disorders, three in particular demonstrate depressive qualities; they are the dependent, the histrionic, and the borderline personality. Critical in dependent personalities' propensity toward depression are their beliefs that they are ineffective, inferior, and unworthy of regard. Depression in the dependent personality manifests itself as helplessness with a poor self-concept and the inability to function autonomously. Millon and Kotik (1985) assert that this negative view of the world is central to Aaron Beck's cognitive theory of depression. Histrionic personalities' extreme need for attention and approval lend themselves to feelings of depression when their needs are not met. Millon and Kotik (1985) state that there may be the presence of underlying depression which is obscured in the histrionic by their dramatic behavioral styles. The borderline personality is characterized by intense mood swings and dependence on others with strong contradictory feelings such as love, rage, and shame. Grinker, Werble, and Drye (1968) in their research study on the borderline personality discuss depression in all of the four borderline subtypes:

> The Group I patients characterized by inappropriate and negative behaviors as well as hostile, angry depression; the Group II or "core" borderlines exhibiting a vacillating involvement with others and acting out of expressions of anger, alternating with a lonely, hopeless depression; the Group III's schizoid personality, with a withdrawn, affectless depression; and the Group IV borderlines characterized by gross defects in self-esteem and confidence and a depressive quality not associated with anger or guilt feelings. (p. 729)

Of the models to be examined, Beck's cognitive model of depression proposes that depression is primarily a result of the tendency to view the self, the future, and the world in an unrealistically negative manner (Sacco and Beck, 1985). More specifically mentioned in Billings and Moos' (1985) article, "Psychosocial Stressors, Coping, and Depression," Beck's theory suggests that "persons with a strong predisposition to assume personal responsibility for negative outcomes are prone to depression; they are filled with self-blame that may cause depression and their pessimistic view of their future effectiveness can adversely affect their coping responses" (p. 947).

The learned helplessness model, however, proposes that at the core of many forms of depression is an expectation of response-outcome independence engendered by experience with uncontrolled events (Peterson & Seligman, 1985). Billings and Moos (1985) suggest that merging these models would create "the paradoxical situation of individuals blaming themselves for outcomes they believe they neither caused nor controlled" (p. 947). In addition, the learned helplessness model introduces the question of sex differences. Wing and Bebbington (1985) concur that depressive disorders are more common in women than in men and further suggest that young, married women with small children are particularly at risk for depression.

Gender difference and depression have long been the topic for research studies. Billings and Moos (1985) report that, "depression is more common among women than among men, but the determinants of this gender difference remain controversial" (p. 960). However, Lin, Woelfel, and Dumin (1986) suggest that the possibility for this finding may be that women are more interested in health and are, therefore, more likely to report symptoms. Men, on the other hand, are less willing to view themselves as being depressed and, therefore, less willing to acknowledge symptoms.

Cermak (1986) suggests that codependents experience depression as evidence of inadequacy and the failure to stay in control as they turn their anger inward, repress unresolved grief, and chronically restrain their feelings. Furthermore, he denotes denial as being characteristic for codependents. Admitting that one is depressed means admitting that one has needs, and co-dependents, by definition, always place the needs of others above their own in importance.

METHODOLOGY

The findings of this study are based on a sample of 149 individuals who completed two self-inventories: The Beck Depression Inventory and an Awareness Activity: How Codependent Are You? All information was obtained anonymously. The only identifying information on each inventory was the individual's sex, age, and marital status.

Instruments

The Beck Depression Inventory (BDI) is a screening tool that determines an individual's level of depression based on his feeling state. Each section of the multiple choice questionnaire is read by the individual and a circle is put around the number next to the answer that best reflects how he has been feeling during the preceding week. Each question is given five possible choices, each choice assigned a weight of zero, one, two, or three points. Scoring consists of adding up the numbers. Based on the total score, individuals are categorized into five levels of depression ranging from normal to severe depression. The reliability and validity of the BDI is well established, indicating a consistent relationship between BDI scores and a person's depressive state.

The "Awareness Activity: How Codependent Are You?" (see Appendix A) was constructed by Robert Edwards, doctoral student, for the purpose of measuring an individual's level of codependency. He adapted two instruments: (1) the 16 Personality Factor Questionnaire (16 PF) developed by Raymond B. Cattell, Ph.D, D.Sc. and IPAT staff and; (2) the Self-Esteem Questionnaire developed by Barry K. Weinhold, Ph.D. (Weinhold and Weinhold, 1989).

The 16 PF is a test of normal adult personality that measures levels of assertiveness, emotional maturity, shrewdness, self-sufficiency, tension, and eleven other primary traits. Edwards used eight construct-selected scales of the 16 PF and converted them to codependent categories based on Cermak's proposed DSM III category. Edwards then administered Weinhold's self-esteem Questionnaire to the same population. He had an across the category's correlation of the 16 PF to the Weinhold Questionnaire of .891.

The Awareness Activity: How Codependent Are You? is a multiple choice questionnaire. Twenty statements are read by the individual and a number from one to four is selected to indicate the degree of agreement. Scoring consists of adding up the numbers. Based on the total score, individuals are categorized into four levels of codependency ranging from a very high degree of codependency patterns to a few codependency patterns.

Subjects and Procedure

Permission was granted to conduct this study by the institutions involved. The individuals who volunteered to complete the inventories were selected from three clinical settings in the New Orleans area:

Group I–The Centers for Psychotherapy (The Westbank Center and The Slidell Center) are private mental health centers staffed by psychiatrists, psychologists, clinical social workers and educational consultants. During the month of July 1990, clients were asked at the time of their initial appointment to complete the two inventories. Forty-one clients completed the inventories; all were usable.

Group II–Northshore Psychiatric Hospital, a private inpatient facility, held a community education program entitled "Sexuality and Spirituality" on July 5, 1990. Forty-one participants completed the inventories; thirty-six were usable.

Group III–New Freedom Inc. is a private outpatient clinic that offers psychological and educational services for the treatment of alcoholism and chemical dependency. They sponsored two community education programs at Southern Baptist Hospital on August, 15, 1990 and September 19, 1990. The topic of the program on August 15th was "Conflict Resolution" and on September 19th was "The Art of Successful Communication." Combining these two programs, 101 participants completed inventories; seventy-two were usable.

RESULTS

Results of this study are based on 149 paired inventories obtained from three clinical settings. A composite score was derived from the sum of the twenty items on the codependency inventory and was used to assess the level of codependency. An index of depression was derived from a composite that subjects gave in response to the Beck Depression Inventory. The major focus of this study was to investigate a correlation between codependency and depression. The resulting data are summarized in Table 1. There was a strong, positive correlation between the two variables, codependency and depression, of .5966 ($p < .00001$), meaning that approximately 36

TABLE 1

Summary of Data

	N̲ Sample	BDI[a]	Codependence[a]
Total	149*	12.81*	49.54*
Group I	41	11.69	48.33
Group II	36	12.76	47.13
Group III	72	13.43	51.47
Female	102	14.02	51.28
Male	47	10.17	45.62

Note.

Group I   Westbank and Slidell Centers for Psychotherapy

Group II   Northshore Psychiatric Hospital Program on Sexuality/Spirituality

Group III   New Freedom Inc. Programs (2)

[a]   Mean Value

*   Correlation between codependency and depression.

R̲ = .5966, p̲ < .00001.

percent of the variance in codependency (the criterion) was accounted for by BDI (the predictor).

When the relationship between codependency and depression was assessed for each of the separate groups, the same trend prevailed across all three groups. There was a correlation of .5537 between codependency and depression in Group I, and correlations of .5726 and .6509 between the same two variables in Group II and Group III respectively. The largest correlation did not differ significantly from the smaller (p = .2246 in the test for difference between independent correlations), suggesting that the positive relationship between the two variables was essentially uniform over the three groups.

The total codependency scores for the three groups were compared. An analysis of variance (ANOVA) showed that the dif- ferences between the groups on codependency was not significant.

The relationship between a measure of codependency and gender was also examined (see Table 1). The females averaged 51.31 while the males averaged 45.57; a statistically significant difference (t (147) = 2.950, p = .0036) (see Figures 1 & 2).

The composite scores derived for each subject on the BDI were also not significantly different across the three groups (see Table 1). The composite scores for both codependency and depression were essentially the same for all three groups. Similarly, the correlation between the two variables was essentially the same across the three groups as well as for the genders (see Figures 3, 4 & 5). In addition, a post hoc comparison was made between the genders in the measure of depression (see Table 1). A significant difference was not found (see Figures 6 & 7). In comparing the relationship of codependency and depression, there was not a significant difference for the predictor variables of either marital status or age.

The internal consistency of the codependency inventory was quantified from the data by means of both a matrix of simple correlations between each of the twenty items on the inventory, the total score, and Chronbach's coefficient alpha, which measures the split-halves reliability of a test. All of the simple correlations between individual items and the total were positive, suggesting that each individual item made a positive contribution to the composite score. The average of the intercorrelation was .3965 which indicates a significant r of .1935 (p < .05). This further attests to the internal consistency of the inventory.

Chronbach's alpha uses the variance of the composite of the 20 scores, and the variances of sub-composites, derived from subsets of the total set of items. Chronbach's alpha for these data was found to be .48, which attests to the internal consistency of the twenty items that comprise the codependency inventory. The first sub-composite for codependency was derived by adding the ten odd-num-

FIGURE 1. FEMALE

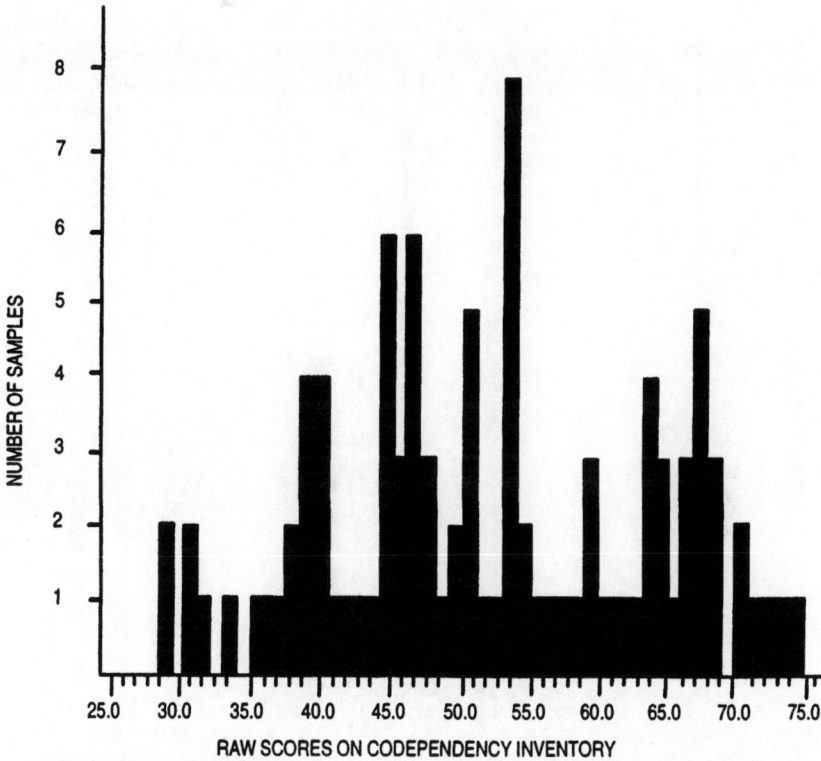

RAW SCORES ON CODEPENDENCY INVENTORY

Frequency Distribution of Codependency for Females: Number of Women who Tested at the Codependent Level Indicated.

bered items and the second sub-composite for codependency was derived by adding the ten even-numbered items. The correlation between the two sub-composites was .9138, and the correlations of each sub-composites with the total score were .9755 and .9735 for sub-composites one and two with the total, respectively.

DISCUSSION

Our first hypothesis was that there would be a positive correlation between a measure of depression and a measure of codependency. The results of this study confirm our hypothesis. While one

FIGURE 2. MALE

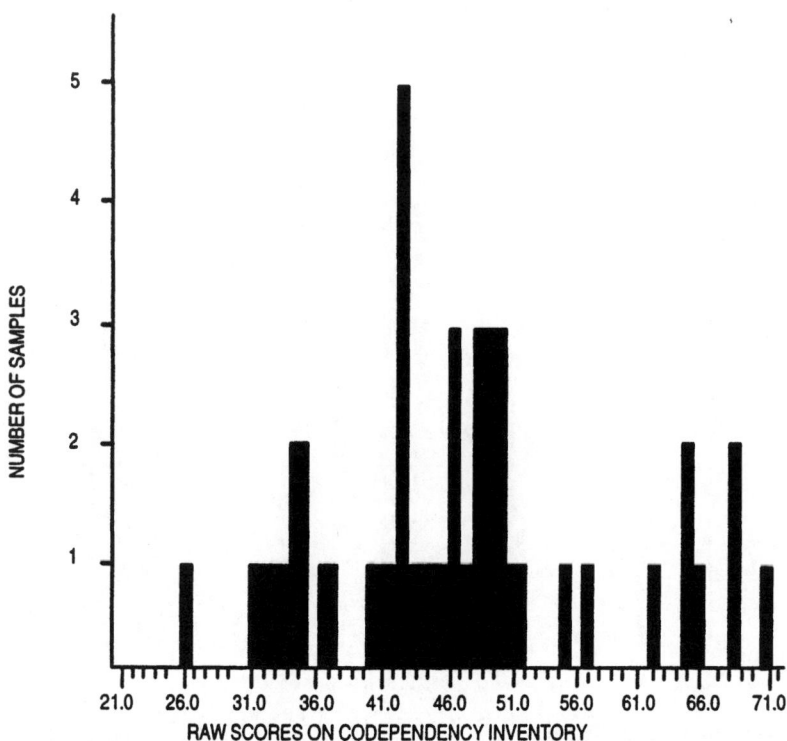

Frequency Distribution of Codependency for Males: Number of Males who Tested at the Codependent Level Indicated.

cannot conclude from this study that codependency and depression are equal, one may suggest that a relationship exists between them. These findings indicate that if a person reports himself/herself to be highly codependent, he/she is likely to experience an elevated level of depression. The degree to which codependency and depression relate would need to be addressed in further research efforts.

When one starts to look at a positive correlation between a measure of codependency and a measure of depression, the possibility of dysfunctional patterns emerge. Millon and Kotik (1985) suggest a relationship exists between personality patterns and the susceptibility

FIGURE 3. RESEARCH SAMPLE

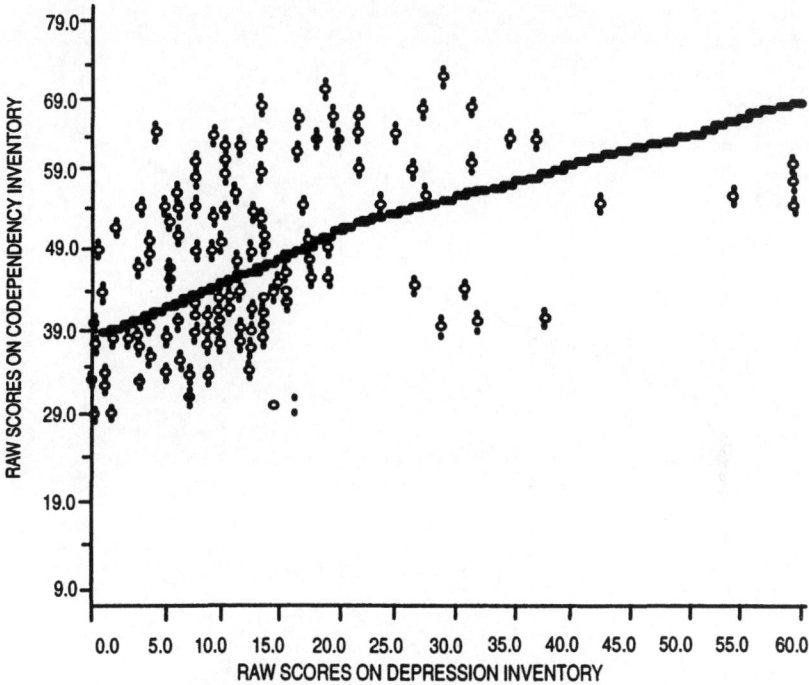

Codependency as a Function of Depression in both Genders:
Individual raw scores for both the Beck Depression Inventory and the Codependency Inventory.

for the development of depressive symptoms. These dysfunctional patterns may give rise to the development of personality disorders. In reviewing the literature on the relationship of depression to personality disorders, one may question whether personality patterns establish a susceptibility to the development of codependency traits as they do to the development of depressive symptoms. Further, is there a positive correlation between a measure of codependency and a measure of personality disorders? The literature review suggests that depression is an integral part of personality disorders such as the histrionic, borderline, and dependent personality. Is it also possible that depression is an integral part of codependency?

FIGURE 4. MALE

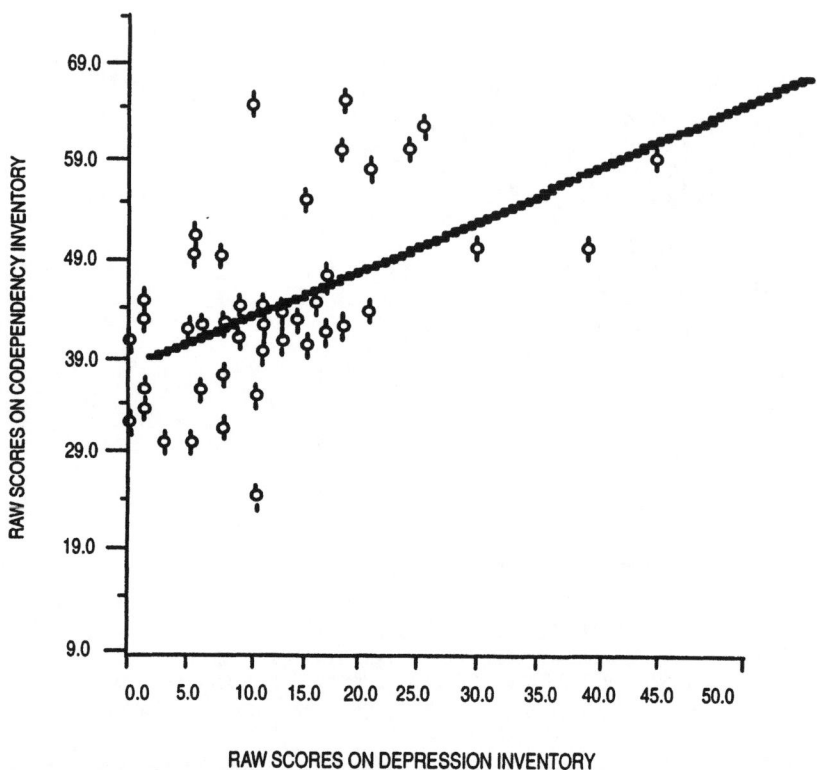

RAW SCORES ON DEPRESSION INVENTORY

Codependency as a function of Depression in Males: Individual raw scores of men for both the Beck Depression Inventory and the Codependency Inventory.

This study may give further credence to Shaw et al. who reported the idea that depression may not be a primary disorder but rather a concomitant disorder; in this case depression in relation to codependency. One area of further research may include looking at codependency levels in patients already diagnosed as being depressed; the reverse of this may also prove useful.

Our study also tested the internal reliability and validity of The Awareness Activity: How Codependent Are You? This study supported the validity of this inventory. By empirically testing the

FIGURE 5. FEMALE

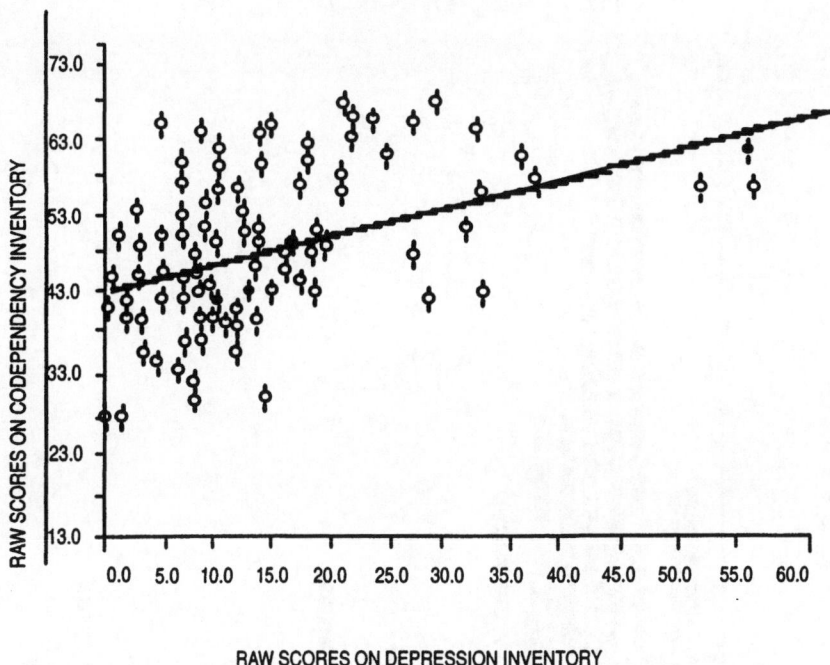

RAW SCORES ON DEPRESSION INVENTORY

Codependency as a Function of Depression in Females: Individual raw scores of women for both the Beck Depression Inventory and the Codependency Inventory.

reliability and validity of the codependency inventory and by suggesting that a positive correlation exists between a measure of codependency and a measure of depression, a step may have been taken towards meeting Cermak's diagnostic criteria for Codependent Personality Disorder. This is beyond the scope of this paper. However, further research in this area may place codependency within the framework of DSM-III-R Personality Disorders.

Our second hypothesis was that women would show a higher statistically significant degree of codependency than men. The results of this study confirm our hypothesis, suggesting that women are more codependent than men. Epstein and Epstein (1990) describe codependency as obtaining one's own sense of self from nurturing and caring for others. They state that the codependent

FIGURE 6. FEMALE

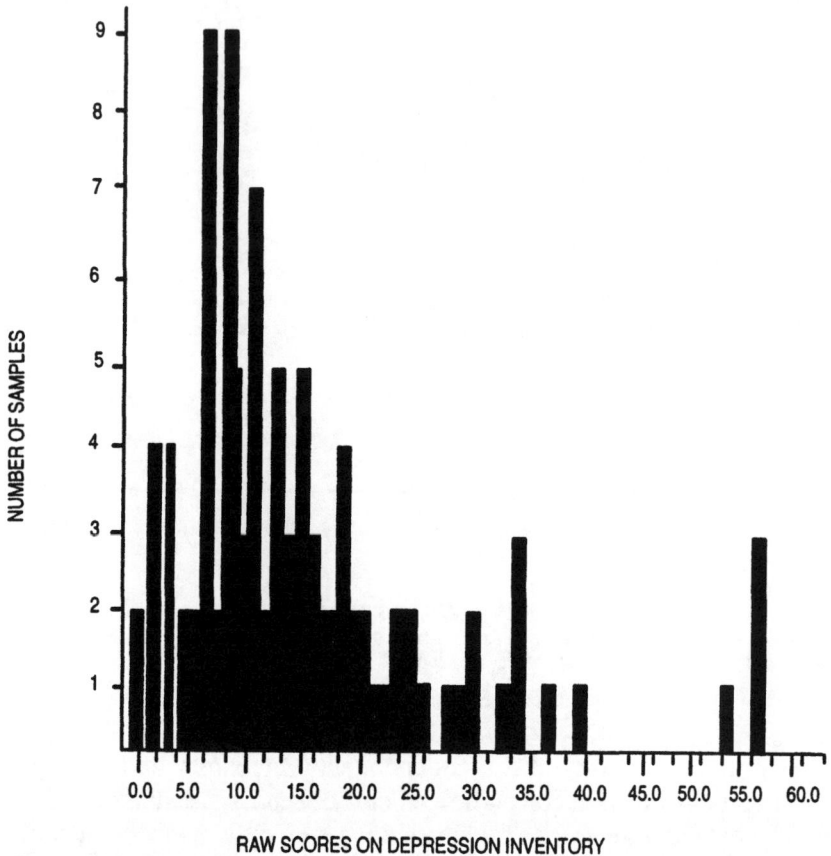

RAW SCORES ON DEPRESSION INVENTORY

Frequency Distribution of Depression for Females: Number of women who Tested at the Depression Level Indicated.

population is primarily composed of women. Our study, however, suggested that both men and women can have a high degree of codependency; although women showed a higher statistically significant degree of codependency than men.

We also decided post hoc to compare the levels of depression between men and women. Billings and Moos (1985) and Lin et al. (1986) report finding a higher level of depression in women than

FIGURE 7. MALE

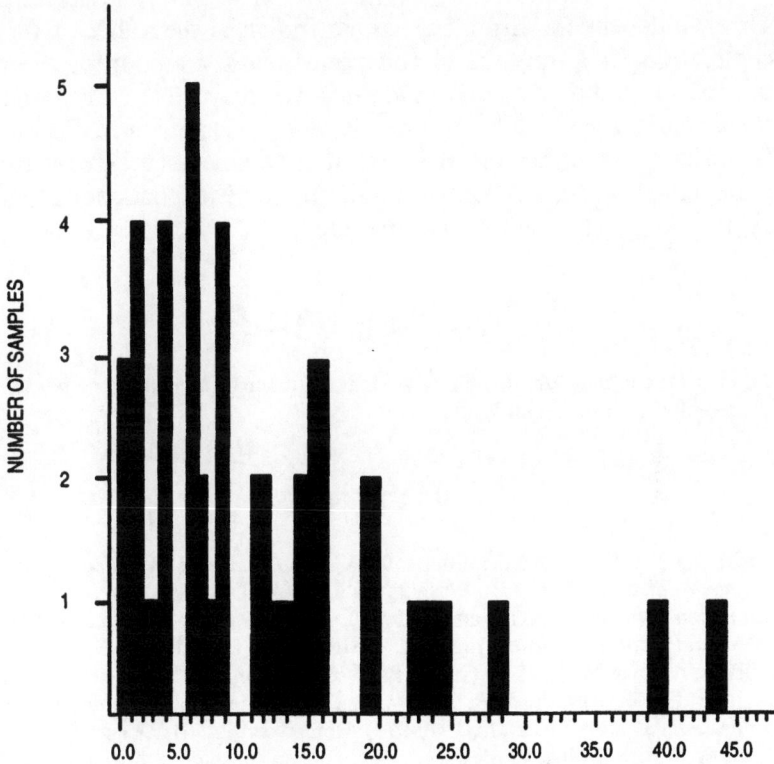

RAW SCORES ON DEPRESSION INVENTORY
Frequency Distribution of Depression for Males: Number of Males who Tested at the Depression Level
Indicated.

men. However, our study did not confirm their findings which may
raise the question of why the results of our study were different.
Perhaps the variance is due to the constraints of our sampling technique; the population of men tested being more health conscious
than that of the general population. Consequently, the outcome of
our study may have been different if a random sample had been
used. In our study, the sample was individuals who showed an

interest in their symptomatology. This may indicate that further research should include a random sample.

This study supported the validity of The Awareness Activity: How Codependent Are You? which indicates the value of further replications as a measure of codependency. By supporting the reliability and validity of this inventory, we may have contributed to the empirical legitimacy of a measure of codependency. Therefore, in order to facilitate the process of assessment and treatment of codependency, further research utilizing the codependency inventory as a diagnostic tool is recommended.

AUTHOR NOTE

This article was submitted in partial fulfillment of the requirements for the degree of Master of Social Work.

REFERENCES

American Psychiatric Association. (1980). *Diagnostic and statistical manual of mental disorders* (3rd ed.). Washington, DC.: Author

American Psychiatric Association. (1987). *Diagnostic and statistical manual of mental disorders* (3rd ed.-revised). Washington, DC: Author

Billings, A. G. & Moos, R. H. (1985). Psychosocial stressors, coping and depression. In E. E. Beckham & W. R. Leber (Eds.), *Handbook of depression: Treatment, assessment, and research* (pp. 940-974). Homewood IL: The Dorsey Press.

Cermak, T. L. (1986). *Diagnosing and treating co-dependence*. Minneapolis: Johnston Institute Books.

Cermak, T. L. (1986). Diagnostic criteria for codependency. *Journal of Psychoactive Drugs. 18*(1), 15-20.

Epstein, M. K., & Epstein, E. K. (1990). Codependence as social narrative. *Readings: A Journal of Reviews and Commentary in Mental Health, 5*(3), 4-7.

Grinker, R. R., Werble, B., Drye, R. C. (1968). *Borderline Syndrome*. New York: Basic Books.

Horney, K. (1950). *Neurosis in human growth*. New York: Norton.

Lin, N., Woelfel, M., & Dumin, M. (1986). Gender of the confident and depression. In N. Lin, A. Dean & W. Ensel (Eds.), *Social support, life events, and depression* (pp. 283-306). Orlando, FL: Academic Press Inc.

Mendenhall, W. (1989). Co-dependency definitions and dynamics. *Alcoholism Treatment Quarterly. 6*(1), 3-17.

Mendenhall, W. (1989). Co-dependency treatment. *Alcoholism Treatment Quarterly. 6*(1), 75-86.

Millon, T. (1981). *Disorders of personality: DSM-III Axis II.* New York: Wiley-Interscience.

Millon, T. & Kotik, D. (1985). The relationship of depression to disorders of personality. In E. E. Beckham & W. R. Leber (Eds.), *Handbook of depression: Treatment, assessment, and research* (pp. 700-744). Homewood IL: The Dorsey Press.

Peterson, C. & Seligman, M. E. P. (1985). The learned helplessness model of depression: Current status of theory and research. In E. E. Beckham & W. R. Leber (Eds.), *Handbook of depression: Treatment, assessment, and research* (pp. 914-939). Homewood IL: The Dorsey Press.

Potter-Efron, R. T. & Potter-Efron, P. S. (1989). Assessment of co-dependency with individuals from alcoholic and chemically dependent families. *Alcoholism Treatment Quarterly.* 6(1), 37-57.

Sacco, W. P. & Beck, A. T. (1985). Cognitive therapy of depression. In E. E. Beckham & W. R. Leber (Eds.), *Handbook of depression: Treatment, assessment, and research* (pp. 3-38). Homewood IL: The Dorsey Press.

Shaw, B. F., Vallis, M., & McCabe, S. B. (1985). The assessment of the severity and symptom patterns in depression. In E. E. Beckham & W. R. Leber (Eds.), *Handbook of depression: Treatment, assessment, and research* (pp. 372-407). Homewood IL: The Dorsey Press.

Smally, S. & Coleman, E. (1987). Treating intimacy dysfunctions in dyadic relationships among chemically dependent and codependent clients. *Journal of Chemical Dependency Treatment.* 1(1), 229-243.

Subby, R. (1984). Inside the chemically dependent marriage: Denial and manipulation. In *Co-dependency: An emerging issue* (pp. 25-29). Pompano Beach, FL: Health Communications Inc.

Wegscheider-Cruse, S. (1985). *Choicemaking.* Pompano Beach FL: Health Communications, Inc.

Whitfield, C. L. (1989). Co-dependence: Our most common addiction–some physical, mental, emotional, and spiritual perspectives. *Alcoholism Treatment Quarterly,* 6(1), 19-36.

Wing, J. K. & Bebbington, P. (1985). Epidemiology of depression. In E. E. Beckham & W. R. Leber (Eds.), *Handbook of depression: Treatment, assessment, and research* (pp. 700-744). Homewood IL.: The Dorsey Press.

APPENDIX A

_____MARITAL STATUS_____
_____SEX____
_____AGE____

AWARENESS ACTIVITY: HOW CODEPENDENT ARE YOU?

The following self-inventory may help you determine the degree to which co-dependency is present in your life. Please answer these questions honestly. Usually the first answer that comes to you is the most honest and most accurate.

A SELF-INVENTORY
TYPICAL CHARACTERISTICS OF CO-DEPENDENT PEOPLE

Directions: Place a number from 1 to 4 in the space before each question to indicate the degree of your response.

1 = Never
2 = Occassionally
3 = Frequently
4 = Almost always

( ) I tend to assume responsibility for others feelings and/or behavior.

( ) I have difficulty in identifying my feelings—happy, angry, scared, sad or excited.

( ) I have difficulty expressing my feelings.

( ) I tend to fear or worry how others may respond to my feelings or behavior.

( ) I minimize problems and deny or alter truth about the feelings or behavior of others.

( ) I have difficulty in forming or maintaining close relationships.

( ) I am afraid of rejection.

( ) I am a perfectionist and judge myself harshly.

( ) I have difficulty making decisions.

( ) I tend to be reactive to others rather than to act on my own.

( ) I tend to put other people's wants and needs first.

APPENDIX A (continued)

( ) I tend to value the opinion of others more than my own.

( ) My feelings of worth come from outside myself, through the opinions of other people or from activities that seem to validate my worth.

( ) I find it difficult to be vulnerable and to ask for help.

( ) I deal with issue self-control by attempting to always be in control or, the opposite, by being careful never to be in a position of responsibility.

( ) I am extremely loyal to others, even when that loyalty is unjustified.

( ) I tend to view situations with "all or none" thinking.

( ) I have a high tolerance for inconsistency and mixed messages.

( ) I have emotional crises and chaos in my life.

( ) I tend to find relationships in which I feel "needed" and attempt to keep it that way.

Scoring: Add the numbers to get a total score. Use the following ranges to help interpret your level of co-dependency:

60-80 - A very high degree of co-dependent patterns
40-59 - A high degree of codependent patterns
30-39 - Some degree of co-dependent and/or counter-dependent patterns
20-29 - A few co-dependent and/or a high degree of counter-dependent patterns.

Source: Weinhold, *Breaking Free*, 16.

The Acceptability
of Alternative Treatment Formats
# of Relationship Therapy:
Ratings by Premarital Subjects

Marian R. Flammang
Gregory L. Wilson

SUMMARY. One hundred fifty premarital subjects evaluated the acceptability of alternative therapeutic formats commonly employed in relationship therapy. Unmarried individuals who were currently involved in premarital relationships were randomly assigned to experimental conditions including two types of educational information (descriptive and group-oriented) presented across three treatment formats (i.e., individual, conjoint, and group). The Treatment Evaluation Inventory and the Semantic Differential served as primary dependent variables. Results revealed that conjoint format was most acceptable followed by group and individual, respectively. However, subjects who had been involved in a relationship longer than one year rated the group and conjoint formats as equal in acceptability. Additionally, group-oriented information increased subjects' ratings of group format.

Acceptability refers to the appropriateness, fairness, and intrusiveness of treatment procedures as judged by patients, lay persons,

---

Marian R. Flammang and Gregory L. Wilson are affiliated with Washington State University.

[Haworth co-indexing entry note]: "The Acceptability of Alternative Treatment Formats of Relationship Therapy: Ratings by Premarital Subjects," Flammang, Marian R., and Gregory L. Wilson. Co-published simultaneously in the *Journal of Couples Therapy* (The Haworth Press, Inc.) Vol. 4, No. 1/2, 1993, pp. 129-140; and: *Attraction and Attachment: Understanding Styles of Relationships* (ed: Barbara Jo Brothers) The Haworth Press, Inc., 1993, pp. 129-140. Multiple copies of this article/chapter may be purchased from The Haworth Document Delivery Center [1-800-3-HAWORTH; 9:00 a.m. - 5:00 p.m. (EST)].

and professionals (Kazdin, 1980a). Acceptability is an important criterion for evaluating relationship treatments because it offers a means to discriminate among equally viable treatment formats. Also, highly acceptable treatments may be frequently selected and better adhered to than those which are rated as less acceptable (Pickering, Morgan, Houts, & Rodrigue, 1988; Wilson & Flam-. mang, 1990; Wilson & Wilson, 1991).

Recently, Wilson and Flammang (1990) examined the acceptability of four alternative treatment formats used in the resolution of dysfunction: individual, concurrent, conjoint, and marital group. Subjects were randomly assigned to experimental conditions which included two forms of information (i.e., descriptive versus research-oriented). Conjoint treatment was consistently rated as most acceptable, followed by concurrent, group, and individual, respectively. Interestingly, providing efficacy information about alternative formats did not alter acceptability ratings.

Later, Wilson, Flammang, and Dehle (in press) evaluated three forms of information (i.e., descriptive, research-oriented, and group-oriented) and two differing case histories were presented across the same treatment formats. Again, conjoint treatment format was rated as most acceptable followed by concurrent, group, and individual, respectively. The type of information which was given to subjects did not affect acceptability ratings, neither did varying case histories.

One limitation of the previous relationship acceptability studies is that college students were employed as subjects. There has been considerable controversy over the use of nonclinical populations in acceptability studies. By using distressed and nondistressed premarital individuals as subjects, this study surveyed the population that is most likely to seek relationship therapy for purposes of premarital therapy or relationship enhancement.

Another important question in acceptability research concerns whether the use of educational information influences acceptability ratings. Some acceptability research has produced results revealing that educational information increases acceptability ratings for interventions with children (Von Brock & Elliott, 1987; Tingstrom, 1989; Singh & Katz, 1985). However, marital acceptability research has yet to demonstrate similar findings.

In an attempt to examine the relative influence of educational information presented to premarital subjects, two types of educational information were used in this study: (1) descriptive, which defined the three different formats of relationship therapy; and (2) group-oriented, which summarized the advantages of group relationship therapy. Thus, the current investigation compared the acceptability ratings of distressed and nondistressed premarital subjects who received different forms of information across three commonly employed therapeutic formats.

METHODS

Subjects

One hundred and fifty premarital subjects (75 males and 75 females) who were currently involved in intimate relationships were utilized as participants in this study. Length of relationship ranged from 2 months to 6 years ($M = 1.59$ years, $SD = 1.14$ years). The median length of relationship across subjects was 1 year. These subjects ranged in age from 17 to 39 years ($M = 19.89$, $SD = 2.82$). Fifty subjects (33%) scored in the distressed range on the Dyadic Adjustment Scale. Scores on the Dyadic Adjustment Scale ranged from 77 to 151 points ($M = 108.69$, $SD = 16.28$). Nineteen percent of the subjects had previously participated in therapy. Of those subjects who had previous therapy experience, individual treatment was most common (12%), followed by family treatment (10%). None of the subjects had previously participated in relationship treatment.

Assessment

Dyadic Adjustment Scale (DAS; Spanier, 1976). The DAS is a widely used self-report questionnaire which provides a global measurement of marital or relationship satisfaction. Spanier (1976) reports that the DAS has excellent reliability (Cronbach's alpha = .96) and substantial criterion-related validity as well as construct validity.

Wilson and Bornstein (1986) recommend using the DAS as a screening device to differentiate between satisfied and dissatisfied couples because of its ease of administration, high stability over time, well-established norms, and applicability with unmarried couples. Individuals who scored below 100 points were classified as being in a "distressed" relationship, while those scoring 100 points or more were classified as "nondistressed."

Treatment Evaluation Inventory (TEI; Kazdin, 1980a, 1980b). The TEI consists of 15 items on a seven-point Likert scale which asks subjects to evaluate such factors as the acceptability of treatment, suitability of procedures for the individuals, and the likely effectiveness of the procedures. It was modified so as to conform with an evaluation of relationship therapy. Previous research on the inventory (Kazdin, 1980a, 1980b) has shown that it is able to discriminate between alternative treatments. In an earlier analysis of the TEI, Wilson and Flammang (1991) found the instrument to have high reliability (Cronbach's alpha = .96, split-half reliability = .96). Higher scores on the TEI are representative of greater acceptability.

Semantic Differential (SD; Osgood, Suci, & Tannenbaum, 1957). The form of the SD used in acceptability research consists of 15 bipolar adjectives, rated on a one-to-seven Likert scale. These 15 adjectives are divided into three subscales (Evaluative, Potency, and Activity) each of which consists of 5 adjective pairs. The adjectives which subjects used to rate treatment formats on the Evaluative subscale included good-bad, valuable-worthless. Adjectives comprising the Potency subscale include strong-weak, hard-soft. Adjectives such as active-passive, fast-slow are characteristic of the Activity subscale. Extensive research with the SD indicates that it is a psychometrically sound and reliable instrument. Osgood et al. (1957) reported a test-retest reliability coefficient of .85.

Recently, Wilson and Flammang (1991) found the SD to be highly reliable when used in acceptability research: Evaluative Scale (Cronbach's alpha = .93; split-half reliability = .95), Potency Scale (Cronbach's alpha = .85; split-half reliability = .90), Activity Scale (Cronbach's alpha = .71; split-half reliability = .80). Across all subscales, higher scores are representative of greater endorsement of that particular construct (e.g., "high potency" versus "low potency").

Procedures

Each subject was given instructions explaining the purpose of the study followed by a packet which included a brief description of the three treatments: individual, conjoint and group. Each packet also contained a written description of a couple seeking treatment for relationship dysfunction. Each subject read the first treatment description and then completed the dependent measures for that vignette. When dependent measures for the first treatment were completed, each subject then proceeded to the next treatment description and completed the attached set of questionnaires for that format of intervention. This procedure was followed until all treatment formats had been evaluated by each subject.

Case Description

A case description of a couple seeking relationship therapy was presented to subjects so that they could apply the various treatment formats to this specific case description. The case description was modified from material presented by Nadelson (1978), which was representative of actual clients and problems frequently seen in outpatient clinical settings.

Informational Materials

Two forms of educational information were presented to subjects in order to evaluate the relative influence of descriptive and group-oriented information on acceptability ratings. Descriptive information consisted of a definition of acceptability, a description of its importance in relation to the purpose of the study, and definitions of the three different treatment formats for relationship therapy. The group-oriented information section included the descriptive information and a summary of research findings that detailed the effectiveness of group relationship therapy. Moreover, subjects were told that group treatment provides special opportunities for learning by working with other couples experiencing similar concerns; it also increases the availability and sources of helpful feedback from others; and it can promote positive expectations through witnessing improvements among other couples.

Treatment Conditions

In order to test the relative significance of the various treatment formats, all treatment descriptions included similar content (e.g., behavioral exchange, expressive and receptive communication skills, training in a nine-step problem-solving approach). However, the therapy process (e.g., talking directly to partner in conjoint sessions; sharing information and suggestions with other couples in group format) was varied significantly depending upon the specific format being described. The therapy descriptions were based on the principles of behavioral marital therapy (Jacobson & Margolin, 1979; Bornstein & Bornstein, 1986). The specific focus of successive sessions paralleled the treatment outcome procedures employed by Wilson and his colleagues (Wilson, Bornstein, & Wilson, 1988; Wilson, 1989; Montag & Wilson, 1991). The therapy descriptions were written in such a way as not to identify whether the therapist was male or female. Treatment sessions lasted for 90 minutes per week for a total of 8 weeks in all conditions. A brief sample of the treatment description follows.

Individual Treatment. Following the initial interview, the therapist recommended that the female partner be treated individually to more directly address her underlying depression, which co-existed with the couple's marital distress. Specifically, therapy focused on several causes of her depression. Treatment strategies included activity scheduling and increasing rates of pleasant events in her daily life. In addition, the couple was told that the female partner would describe the package of relationship techniques and strategies that she learned in therapy to her partner at home.

Conjoint Treatment. During conjoint sessions, the therapist facilitated a dialogue between the couple. The therapist provided feedback concerning their use of communication and conflict resolution skills that were exhibited in session. Both partners met with the therapist for every session.

Group Treatment. The couple was described as participating in a group with four other couples who were attempting to improve their relationships. Group interactions incorporated feedback from participants and the therapist in communication tactics and problem-solving strategies.

RESULTS

The scores of the TEI and the SD-Evaluative Scale were analyzed as a summed score because they were found to be highly intercorrelated. Pearson product-moment correlation coefficients of these two dependent measures ranged from .75 to .85 (*ps* < .001). Likewise, the SD-Activity and Potency Scales were summed, correlation coefficients ranged from .58 to .64 (*ps* < .001). These dependent measures were summed because they cannot be regarded as independent measures, and the combined score taps more of the true variance of the construct of acceptability than does either score alone.

An initial 2 × 3 (Level of Distress × Treatment Format) series of univariate analyses of variance (ANOVAs) were conducted and failed to reveal significant findings for the Level of Distress main effect or the Level of Distress × Treatment Format interaction. Therefore, we collapsed across Level of Distress for all remaining analyses.

Results were analyzed via a 2 × 2 × 2 × 3 (Information × Gender of Subject × Length of Relationship × Treatment Format) multivariate analysis of variance (MANOVA), with repeated measures on the final factor, across all dependent variables. Subjects were divided into long-term (over 1 year) and short-term (less than 1 year) length of relationship based on a median split procedure.

The MANOVA showed a significant main effect for Treatment Format, Wilks's lambda = .53, F (4, 139) = 30.61, p < .001. In addition, a significant Information × Treatment Format interaction was revealed, Wilks's lambda = .93, F (4, 139) = 2.76, p < .05. A significant Length of Relationship × Treatment Format interaction was also observed, Wilks's lambda = .91, F (4, 139) = 3.60, p < .01. All other main effects and interactions proved nonsignificant. Summary data for each dependent variable across treatment format are presented in Table 1.

Subsequent ANOVAs on dependent variables revealed significant Treatment Format main effects on the combined TEI/SD-Evaluative Scale, F (2, 284) = 55.81, p < .001; and on the combined SD-Potency/Activity Scale, F (2, 284) = 32.91, p < .001. Neuman-Keuls multiple comparison tests on both the combined TEI/SD-Evaluative Scale and the combined SD-Potency/Activity Scale revealed that all treatment formats were rated as significantly different from one another with conjoint treatment format being evaluated as most acceptable followed by group and individual treatment formats, respectively.

TABLE 1. Comparison of Mean Scores Across Treatment Formats on Each Dependent Measure

		Conjoint	Group	Individual
TEI/SD - Evaluative***				
	M	105.91[a]	96.25[b]	80.13[c]
	SD	18.69	22.24	26.44
SD - Potency/Activity***				
	M	46.80[a]	44.57[b]	39.23[c]
	SD	8.98	8.85	9.74

*** = .001 level of significance.

Mean scores that share a common superscript are not significantly different.

Subsequent ANOVAs also demonstrated a significant Length of Relationship × Treatment Format interaction on the TEI/SD-Evaluative Scale, F (2, 284) = 7.25, $p < .01$; and on the SD-Potency/Activity Scale, F (2, 284) = 4.35, $p < .05$. Neuman-Keuls analyses demonstrated that subjects who had been in a relationship longer than 1 year rated the group and conjoint treatment formats as equal in acceptability as measured by both the TEI/SD-Evaluative and the SD-Potency/Activity Scales. The individual treatment format was rated as least acceptable on both measures. Additionally, subjects who were involved in a relationship less than 1 year rated the individual treatment format as significantly more acceptable than did subjects who had been involved in relationship for longer than 1 year. Summary data for the Length of Relationship × Treatment Format interaction is presented in Table 2.

ANOVAs also revealed a significant Information × Treatment Format interaction on the TEI/SD-Evaluative Scale, F (2, 284) = 3.86, $p < .05$. Neuman-Keuls analyses showed that when group-oriented information was given to subjects, the conjoint and group formats were found to be equivalent and both were rated as more acceptable than individual treatment. All other main effects and interactions proved nonsignificant. Summary data for the Information × Treatment Format interaction is presented in Table 3.

Finally, subjects were also given the opportunity to indicate treatment format preference ratings. Once again, these results clearly indicated the superiority of conjoint (n = 85), followed by group (n = 49), and individual (n = 16), *Chi Square* = 47.64, *df* = 2, *p* < .001.

In order to evaluate the relative influence of previous therapy experience on acceptability ratings of alternative relationship formats, a series of 2 × 3 (Previous Therapy Experience × Treatment Format) posthoc ANOVAs were completed. No interaction or main effect involving previous therapy was found. Subjects were also asked to rate themselves in terms of their likelihood to participate in relationship therapy. Fifty-one percent rated themselves as being likely to participate, 20% rated themselves as unlikely, and 29% remained uncommitted.

TABLE 2. Comparison of Mean Scores Across Treatment Format as a Function of Length of Relationship

		Conjoint		Group		Individual	
		Longer Term	Shorter Term	Longer Term	Shorter Term	Longer Term	Shorter Term
TEI/SD - Evaluative**							
	M	107.46[a]	104.39[a]	100.77[a]	91.84[b]	75.30[c]	84.61[d]
	SD	18.51	18.86	22.66	21.05	25.06	27.10
SD - Potency/Activity*							
	M	46.77[a]	46.83[a]	45.49[a]	43.68[ab]	37.28[c]	41.13[b]
	SD	9.62	8.38	9.22	8.43	9.74	9.42

* = .05, ** = .01 level of significance.

Mean scores that share a common superscript are not significantly different.

TABLE 3. Comparison of Mean Scores Across Treatment Format as a Function of Information

	Conjoint		Group		Individual	
	Descriptive	Group-Oriented	Descriptive	Group-Oriented	Descriptive	Group-Oriented
TEI/SD - Evaluative*						
M	107.43[a]	104.42[a]	91.18[b]	101.18[a]	76.86[c]	83.08[c]
SD	19.62	17.73	21.63	21.85	26.62	26.08

* = .05 level of significance.

Mean scores that share a common superscript are not significantly different.

DISCUSSION

The results of this study clearly indicate that: (a) conjoint treatment format was generally rated as most acceptable, followed by group and individual interventions, respectively; (b) similarly, when asked to choose between the three therapy formats, significantly more subjects chose the conjoint condition as the most preferred format; (c) subjects who had been involved in a relationship longer than one year rated group and conjoint treatment formats as equal in acceptability; (d) additionally, subjects who had been involved in a relationship less than one year rated the individual treatment format as significantly more acceptable than did all other subjects; (e) educational information appears to influence acceptability ratings in that subjects who received group-oriented information rated group treatment as more acceptable than did subjects who received only descriptive information.

In previous acceptability studies regarding relationship treatment formats, educational information did not influence acceptability ratings (Wilson & Flammang, 1990; Wilson, Flammang, & Dehle, in press). However, these studies employed college students as subjects. Thus, it appears that the response to educational information differs between premarital individuals and college students. One reason for this finding may be that individuals currently involved in relationships found the educational information more salient. Moreover, a significant percentage of the premarital subjects in this study (51%) rated themselves as being likely to participate in relationship therapy. Therefore, it may be assumed that premarital subjects have higher levels of anticipated involvement in relationship therapy than do college students, and thus, educational information may be more relevant for premarital subjects.

Choice of treatment format is an important consideration because it influences the outcome of treatment interventions (Beutler & Clarkin, 1990). Since all of the subjects who participated in this study were involved in intimate relationships, these results provide valuable information which may help clinicians decide which format of relationship therapy to offer clients.

AUTHOR NOTE

This research is part of the dissertation project that Marian R. Flammang completed as partial fulfillment for the doctor of philosophy degree at Washington State University. Gratitude is expressed to Herb Cross, and James Whipple who served on her committee. Address correspondence to Marian R. Flammang, M.S., Department of Psychology, Washington State University, Pullman, WA 99164-4820.

REFERENCES

Beutler, L. E., & Clarkin, J. F. (1990). *Systematic treatment selection: Toward targeted therapeutic interventions.* New York: Brunner/Mazel.

Bornstein, P. H., & Bornstein, M. T. (1986). *Marital therapy: A behavioral-communications approach.* New York: Pergamon Press.

Jacobson, N. S., & Margolin, G. (1979). *Marital therapy: Strategies based on social learning and behavior exchange principles.* New York: Brunner/Mazel.

Kazdin, A.E. (1980a). Acceptability of alternative treatments for deviant child behavior. *Journal of Applied Behavior Analysis, 13,* 259-273.

Kazdin, A. E. (1980b). Acceptability of time out from reinforcement procedures for disruptive child behavior. *Behavior Therapy, 11,* 329-344.

Montag, K., & Wilson, G. L. (1991). *An empirical evaluation of behavioral and cognitive-behavioral group marital treatments with rural couples.* Submitted for publication.

Nadelson, C. C. (1978). Marital therapy from a psychoanalytic perspective. In T. J. Paolino and B. S. McCrady (Eds.), *Marriage and marital therapy: Psychoanalytic, behavioral, and systems theory perspectives.* New York: Brunner/Mazel.

Osgood, C.E., Suci, G. J., & Tannenbaum, P. H. (1957). *Measurement of meaning.* Urbana, IL: University of Illinois Press.

Pickering, D., Morgan, S. B., Houts, A. C., & Rodrigue, J. R. (1988). Acceptability of treatments for self-abuse: Do risk-benefit information and being a parent make a difference? *Journal of Clinical Child Psychology, 17,* 209-216.

Singh, N. N. & Katz, R. C. (1985). On the modification of acceptability ratings for alternative child treatments. *Behavior Modification, 9,* 375-386.

Spanier, G. B. (1976). Measuring dyadic adjustment: New scales for assessing the quality of marriage and similar dyads. *Journal of Marriage and the Family, 38,* 15-28.

Tingstrom, D. H. (1989). Increasing acceptability of alternative behavioral interventions through education. *Psychology in the Schools, 26,* 188-194.

Von Brock, M. B., & Elliott, S. N. (1987). The influence of treatment effectiveness information on the acceptability of classroom intervention. *Journal of School Psychology, 25,* 131-144.

Wilson, G. L. (1989, November). The empirical status of alternative treatment formats in behavioral marital therapy. In N. S. Jacobson (Chair), *New Developments in the Behavioral Prevention & Treatment of Marital Discord.* Symposium presented at the annual convention of the Association for the Advancement of Behavior Therapy, Washington, D.C.

Wilson, G. L., & Bornstein, P. H. (1986). The assessment of marital interaction. In P. H. Bornstein & M. T. Bornstein (Eds.), *Marital therapy: A behavioral-communications approach.* New York: Pergamon Press.

Wilson, G. L., Bornstein, P. H., & Wilson, L. J. (1988). Treatment of relationship dysfunction: An empirical evaluation of group and conjoint behavioral marital therapy. *Journal of Consulting and Clinical Psychology, 56,* 929-931.

Wilson, G. L., & Flammang, M. R. (1990). Treatment acceptability of alternative formats of marital therapy. *Scandinavian Journal of Behaviour Therapy, 19,* 87-99.

Wilson, G. L., & Flammang, M. R. (1991). *Psychometric characteristics of acceptability measures: A comparison of the Treatment Evaluation Inventory and the Semantic Differential.* Unpublished manuscript.

Wilson, G. L., Flammang, M. R., & Dehle, C. M. (in press). Therapeutic formats in the resolution of relationship dysfunction: An acceptability investigation. *Journal of Sex and Marital Therapy.*

Wilson, G. L., & Wilson, L. J. (1991). Treatment acceptability of alternative sex therapies: A comparative analysis. *Journal of Sex and Marital Therapy, 17,* 35-44.

Change, Vulnerability, Fear,
and Taking Risks–
An Interview with Virginia Satir

Sheldon Starr

[Early in 1985 I asked Virginia Satir if she was willing to be interviewed on videotape concerning her thinking about family therapy at that time and especially with regard to any ideas she might wish to share with the family therapy community. The interview took place on March 15, 1985 at Virginia's home in Menlo Park, California. The transcript of the interview is 60 pages, and this is the *sixth and final one* of a series of segments from that interview covering different themes.]

[The use of brackets [ ] and underlining below are editorial additions for the purpose of clarity and/or emphasis.] S.S.

Sheldon Starr, PhD, was founder and director for 15 years of the Family Study Unit, a family therapy training and treatment program at the V.A. Medical Center, Palo Alto, CA when this interview was conducted. Dr. Starr is presently Professor of Psychology (part time) at Pacific Graduate School of Psychology and is in private practice, both in Palo Alto, CA. His association with Virginia Satir spanned 25 years, first as student, then as associate and long-time friend. Correspondence may be sent to 770 Welch Road, #161, Palo Alto, CA 94304.

A highly condensed and edited summary of the entire interview appeared in the AFTA Newsletter, Fall 1985 and that version consisted of less than 20% of the interview.

[Haworth co-indexing entry note]: "Change, Vulnerability, Fear, and Taking Risks–An Interview with Virgnia Satir," Starr, Sheldon. Co-published simultaneously in the *Journal of Couples Therapy* (The Haworth Press, Inc.) Vol. 4, No. 1/2, 1993, pp. 141-45; and: *Attraction and Attachment: Understanding Styles of Relationships* (ed: Barbara Jo Brothers) The Haworth Press, Inc., 1993, pp. 141-145. Multiple copies of this article/chapter may be purchased from The Haworth Document Delivery Center [1-800-3-HAWORTH; 9:00 a.m. - 5:00 p.m. (EST)].

141

STARR: You know there's been a relatively newer sub-specialty in the Family Therapy field called Family Systems Medicine. Family Systems Medicine is maybe a variant of what in the '60's was called, for individuals, Holistic Medicine. Be that as it may, what do you feel and think about the application of Family Systems to strictly medical areas?

SATIR: [I think of] Bill Offencost in 1955. Bill was a medical person and he was at the University of Chicago. In 1955, Bill delivered a paper on treating, the family as the unit of treatment for medical problems. He did a whole lot of work. Somebody came in with some kind of problem, and he did a history and examination of the *whole* family. So it makes absolute and complete sense because the rules in the family are going to manifest themselves in some way. And I think it's absolutely important. When I was working at the Illinois State Psychiatric Institute and training Family Therapists, I was doing something called Family Dynamics in 1955. I read all the cases that came to the State Hospital every month because I was picking out cases for the residents. And I watched the histories of these families because in those days we could get a lot of history and I watched how there would be depression and then some form of acting-out and then some kind of physical illness. Then there might be some gross kind of mental disturbance like paranoia in these families. So it seems to me that it is time that we take a look. I can see it in terms of a cellular wholeness, in any unit, any life unit, every cell carries with it the picture and the ability to develop the whole thing whether it's a dog or human or whatever. It also carries its specific function, it carries both. Alright, what inhibits you from doing your job is a whole of the entire relationship between the thinking, the feeling and the physical reaction. And that's what we call Medicine, the physical reaction of something. All of the things we know about family rules [are] bound to be enlightening for the way in which medical problems emerge in families.

STARR: See I have an opinion, a bias. It's cost efficient to approach a medical problem from a systemic standpoint.

SATIR: Of course it is.

STARR: But what do you think we'd have to do to convince insurance companies who often would have to pay for that. Most insurance companies have cut out Family Therapy benefits. That's rather short sighted I think.

SATIR: Let me tell you something. See you've raised this question in another form several times. That's when I ask myself, "How do I change something?" Just that question. How do I get somebody who's behaving in a certain way to behave another way? What's the difference between getting an insurance company to open up to see what's going on as compared to getting a family to let their kids decide [something]? No difference at all. How do you initiate change? Alright. From where I am the way change gets initiated is that three things have to happen. Someone has to get the insurance companies against the wall so that they then conduct a study from which they would see that treating families would be cheaper than individuals. Then there is a second one which is that there are some enlightened people out there who didn't know for sure how well it was going, but it looked "right" because they were using their [common] sense to do it. Then there will be a number of insurance companies after some of them start, [covering families] that will go along because of the bandwagon. There's a lot of bandwagon business. So what we need to do is some research. A lot of people have this information clinically, and they know it. But a clinical hunch doesn't pass for hard research. So what we need to do is get people to start research on this so that we can show the insurance companies what can really happen.

STARR: Where are we? The kind of person that we're talking about would have to have a good sense of security or self-confidence because I work in a system (Veterans Administration) where people who are in a position to change are too scared. They're frightened and afraid to change.

SATIR: What's different between that and a patient who comes in and says, "I want to change but I'm scared?"

STARR: There is no difference except for prerogatives.

SATIR: I don't see any difference at all. And I face people with that and I pray. So what's wrong with taking a risk and doing what you know fits? See that's exactly what happened in Germany. A lot of people cared [but did nothing].

STARR/SATIR (together): Yeah, but they were too scared.

SATIR: Now what is it that we work on? In fact there's a marvelous book that's coming out. It's called *Dying to Live* and it's written by a man named Telly Birkin. And what he demonstrates so clearly is that fear is more powerful than our common sense. So what we have to do is go beyond fear, and his book is about that. And I highly recommend it to people. *Dying to Live* by Telly Birkin.

STARR: Catchy title.

SATIR: But going on, well that's what he did. He died so he could live. Anyway, the point you're making is a very important one. If I violate my common sense and do something else because I think that somebody will like it or I don't want to be out there vulnerable, then I'm in trouble. See, my history was I didn't do that. I took whatever steps I know how to take. But the reason that I could do that were two. Number one is because I was sort of nice and I didn't make fun of people or put them down because they may have questioned me and so they would come [to therapy]. They were interested. And the other thing was that I worked with the people no one else wanted, so it was too late by the time we got there. But fear is everywhere, and when professionals say to me, "I can't do it because I'm afraid" and when "I'm afraid" translates into "What will they say?", I say, "I don't know what they'll say. Why don't you ask them? But in the meantime, what kind of *prostitution* are you getting into yourself, to say you know something that fits but you don't do it?" And what difference is that?

STARR: Okay. Let me play devil's advocate.

SATIR: Sure.

STARR: Joan of Arc stuck with her principles and she burned at the stake; Galileo recanted, but we still know that the earth is *not* the center of the universe.

SATIR: Okay. Well, that might be the outcome that some of us have to face.

STARR: Well, so what you're saying is that maybe some people don't want to take the lumps.

SATIR: Right.

STARR: They'll go with it and that's an individual choice that people make.

SATIR: We can do more in this context of the world than before [in an earlier era], and there are different ways.

STARR: I believe that. Yeah.

SATIR: (Strongly) Because I think [nowadays] it's more open; it has been more open so we can do more, but the fact of it is, can I guarantee you anything? Nothing. (Strongly and with emotion.) But what is the sense of living with yourself and feeling OK, but that when you turn around you [discover that you are] prostituting yourself!

STARR: Well, okay, yeah, yeah. You're not talking with an adversary because I feel that way also. The VA Family Study Unit in 1970 were treating homosexual couples. We just didn't talk about it publicly because at that point they'd (VA) have killed the program. Now we can do that. You see, now that's out in the open, but we were doing it way back then.

SATIR: We've got more of that, more people need to take risks, and learning how to take risks is important. *Many people behave as though they've only two possibilities, to attack and rebel or capitulate. Those [certainly] are two you can use, but you can also do something quite different.* It's the same thing as when you get a double level message. You can respond to one or the other [level] or simply say you know there are two things here and comment on the presence of what is going on and ask for something else.

An environmentally friendly book printed and bound in England by www.printondemand-worldwide.com

PEFC Certified

This product is
from sustainably
managed forests
and controlled
sources

PEFC
PEFC/16-33-415

www.pefc.org

MIX
Paper from
responsible sources

FSC
www.fsc.org

FSC® C004959

This book is made entirely of sustainable materials; FSC paper for the cover and PEFC paper for the text pages.

#0097 - 280513 - C0 - 229/152/8 [10] - CB